GROWING AND COOKING POTATOES

GROWING AND COOKING

POTATOES

by Mary W. Cornog

YANKEE, Inc.

Dublin, New Hampshire

Designed by Carl Kirkpatrick
Illustrated by Ray Maher

Published 1981

Yankee, Inc., Dublin, New Hampshire 03444

First Edition

© Copyright 1981, by Yankee, Inc.

Printed in the United States of America

Library of Congress Catalog Card No. 80-52993
ISBN 0-911658-15-7

For Michael.

ACKNOWLEDGMENTS

Grateful acknowledgment is made to the Maine Potato Council and Mr. Ed Plissy for assistance, recipes, and raw materials, and to the growers and researchers of Aroostook County for their kind advice and encouragement.

GROWING AND COOKING POTATOES

CONTENTS

INTRODUCTION

Growing your own potatoes is an experience that verges on the mystical. First you enjoy the lush green foliage and the lightly-tinted blossoms, then you unearth the lumpy buried treasure. And finally you taste the tender delight of fresh potatoes — incomparable. Easy to grow, fun to dig, wonderful to have in your cellar into the winter. Plant several varieties for different tastes and textures, and use potatoes in ways you never thought of before. The recipes in this book will encourage your creativity and please your palate all at the same time.

Varieties available for the home grower and sources for them are listed at the end of the "Growing" section — lots of ways to eat them fill the "Cooking" section.

Mary W. Cornog
Dublin, New Hampshire

GROWING AND COOKING POTATOES

GROWING POTATOES

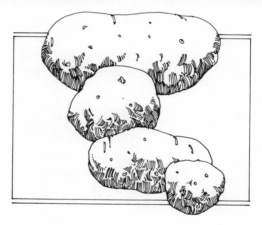

HISTORY AND LORE

He's a meat and potatoes man. One potato, two potato, three potato, four. Five potato, six potato, seven potato, more. You say potayto and I say potahto, so let's call the whole thing off. He dropped her like a hot potato. You missed, you got a D, SPUD you're out. Hamburger and French fries, anywhere in the world. Dancing the Mashed Potato in the '60s.

What do you call a bomb-throwing potato? A pomme de terror.

What do you call a potato that jumps out and kisses girls against their will? A masher.

Who's the hero of the novel set in Chicago? Spuds Lonigan.

What potato started to run for President from the state of Tennessee? Baker.

And on and on and on. Cultural evidence of our attachment to potatoes abounds. No other food is quite like it, or ever had as enormous an effect on the world. For good or, at least once, for ill. Much of the Northern Hemisphere relies on the spud as a dietary staple. The Oriental countries have been the exception, but even they are now taking up potato eating, with Japan in the vanguard.

South America has been firmly convinced of the potato's merits for 2400 years, but that continent had about 1700 years' head start on the rest of the world: potatoes, like squash and corn, were completely unknown to Europeans before the New World came under their sway. In the ancient ruins of highland Peru and Chile, archaeologists have found potato remains that date back to 500 B.C. Completely unknown elsewhere until the late 16th century, the potato, that funny-looking fixture of Western cuisine, began its worldwide career in the Andes Mountains of South America. The Incas who grew and ate them there also worshipped them. Then (as still among the Andean Indian descendants of the Incas) the potato was the main crop and the main food. The Incas buried potatoes with their dead; they stashed potatoes in concealed bins for use in case of war or famine; they dried them and carried them on long treks to eat on the way, dried or soaked in stew. Exceptionally fine tubers were dedicated to the gods to solicit divine favor, and many Incan religious rites and prayers had to do with the planting, growing, and harvesting of potatoes.

Ancient Incan potatoes had dark purplish skins and yellow flesh and flourished naturally in the rocky soils and high elevations of the Andes. The thirty-odd different strains of potatoes grown in highland Peru, Chile, and Bolivia today are direct descendants. And, at least in the very high mountains, farming methods haven't changed much either: poke a hole, stick in the seed potato, harvest later. No plowing, no cultivating, no fuss.

Spanish invaders arriving in search of gold as early as 1524 were the first Europeans to "discover" the potato. But not until Gonzalo Jiminez de Quesada, exhausted and goldless, took it to Spain in lieu of gold did the potato make its official debut on the European scene, sometime between 1565 and 1580. The Spanish regarded the new article as a curiosity rather than a food, and as such the potato was passed on to Italy about 1585, to Belgium and Germany by 1587, to Austria about a year later, and to France around 1600.

The potato's true scientific name is *Solanum tuberosum,* the name bestowed on it by the Swiss botanist Kaspar Bauhin and confirmed by Linnaeus in his 1753 treatise, *Species Plantarum.* This label, used by botanists today, correctly places the potato in the plant family Solanaceae, to which peppers, eggplant, tomatoes, tobacco, petunias, nicotiana, and deadly nightshade also belong.

The Incas called it "papas," as they do today, but an English botanist, attempting in 1597 to define the plant scientifically, mistakenly labeled it *Batata virginiana.* The plant he gave this name was not at all the one he took it for, nor did it come from Virginia, but the English-speaking world and peoples influenced by them derived the name "potato" from his mistake, and the name stuck. The 16th-century botanical confusion about its origins still lingers today among the true potato, several true root vegetables, and the sweet potato.

According to legend, Sir Walter Raleigh first brought the potato to Ireland. But in fact, the plant he took there from England was not a potato at all, but a yam plant Sir Francis Drake had brought from the West in 1586. (When Drake rescued the survivors of the English colony at Roanoke, Virginia, one of the returning colonists packed along a curious root to show his friends back home. In time this man became manager of Sir Walter Raleigh's Irish holdings, where he planted and raised the yam-like tuber. Drawings and descriptions of the plant and its root indicate that it definitely was not what came to be known as the Irish potato.)

Unlike the Incas, Europeans for some reason found the bizarre purplish skin and yellow flesh of the early potato unattractive. So they began experimenting to modify the early types, until they produced potatoes of more uniform shape, with better texture, tougher skin, greater resistance to disease, whiter flesh, browner or redder skin, and a host of other "desirable" characteristics. Ironically enough, scientists today are busily seeking the mountain descendants of the first European potatoes as a source of the original gene material. They now want to breed new varieties with the highly-colored skin and flesh of their Incan ancestors for the South American market.

Despite its high status as a food in the modern world and in ancient Incan lands, the potato met with strong resistance from European eaters. Adoption of the spud as a staple table item took almost two hundred years. Wherever it was introduced — Spain, Holland, Germany, Italy, England, Ireland, France — the potato was considered weird, poisonous, and downright evil. It is, after all, close cousin to the deadly nightshade. It grows not from seed, and its existence is nowhere even hinted at in the Bible. What good could possibly inhere in such an unnatural phenomenon? But the lovely flowers of many shades and the lush green leaves of the potato plant made it irresistible to gardeners and to the ladies of the day, who wore the blossoms in their hair right up to the reign of Queen Marie Antoinette. She often pinned potato flowers in her curls, and it's possible she wore them to the guillotine.

So high had opposition to the potato run that an edict was made in the town of Besançon, France, in 1630 stating: "In view of the fact that the potato is a pernicious substance whose use can cause leprosy, it is hereby forbidden, under pain of fine, to cultivate it." Tomatoes and peppers, also members of the Solanaceae family, were similarly banned.

In France and elsewhere, the potato was variously accused of causing not only leprosy, but also syphilis, narcosis, scrofula, early death, sterility, and rampant sexuality, and of destroying the soil where it grew. In England, a group formed in the late 17th century to campaign against the consumption of potatoes. Called the Society for the Prevention of Unsatisfactory Diets, the group gave its initials — S.P.U.D. — as a nickname to the potato forevermore, but had little effect on the future of its target.

Russian peasants refused to have anything to do with the potato until the mid-1700s. The Swedes, who had been using potatoes only as animal fodder, finally began to eat them themselves in 1771 to stave off famine. Prussian nobles swore they would cut off their vassals' noses and ears if they continued to refuse to grow the vegetable. And back in France documents record at least one instance where the plant and its tubers were punished for crimes against God and man by being burnt at the stake. The French should have sampled the roasted remains.

Such fear and loathing were certainly a far cry from either 2000 years of Incan fascination with the potato, or latter-day infatuation of a good half the world with it. Discovery of the culinary delights of the potato came slowly. Legend says that in France a clever noble helped the process along by posting needless guards over his potato patch to prevent non-existent pilfering. The local peasants, as is only human, decided anything so carefully guarded must be valuable, and they began to steal and eat the noble's potatoes. From this small start, the habit of eating potatoes spread throughout France. French chefs began to discover the endless variety of ways potatoes could be cooked, and nobles began competing for the honor of the newest creation. In the 18th century, the mistress of King Louis XV, the same Madame Pompadour who made the distinctive Pompadour hair style fashionable, created a dish called "potatoes Pompadour." Once Europe began to capitulate, complete surrender was fast.

Once the edibility of the potato was "discovered," it ranked high as a delicacy until it became plentiful. Englishmen once paid as much as $1000 per pound to import it from Ireland. As its popularity blossomed, the potato came to be regarded as a preventive and cure for as many maladies as it was formerly believed to have caused.

Quite correctly, it was used as a cure for scurvy, and lasted better in storage on ocean-going ships than citrus fruits. (Its high vitamin C content is the prophylactic agent.) Less probably, a dried piece suspended from the neck was supposed to cure or prevent rheumatism and sciatica. A raw potato, halved, supposedly cured warts when rubbed against them and then buried, or cut up and tied on them as a poultice. In Holland, potatoes were thought to heal only if stolen from someone else's patch. The folk of Yorkshire, England, insured its curative potency by setting the tuber out in the morning sun to absorb the rays. In parts of Canada, a slice of baked spud was encased in a sock and hung around the neck to cure a sore throat. In the southern United States, grated raw potato was used to soothe burns or frostbite. Half a raw potato drew the swelling and discoloration from a black eye. (This last use seems legitimate — the potato does draw out fluids.) In some parts of Europe, water in which potatoes had been boiled served as a healing balm for aches, sprains, and even broken bones, but washing healthy parts of the body with that water was believed to cause warts. A small stone soaked in potato water and carried in a pocket either prevented ailments or cured them, depending on the bearer's need. And finally, the mashed pulp of a roasted potato was used to treat thrush in horses.

Remnants of the potato's once terrifying reputation persisted for some time. A pot of tubers, boiled and dumped on a neighbor's field, could be counted on to destroy his crop. Sicilians sought revenge by fastening paper inscribed with a hated name to a raw potato with as many pins as possible. Within a month, the bearer of the name was guaranteed to die a hideously painful death. Superstition dies hard.

Nowhere did the potato catch on faster than in Ireland,

where the true potato, *Solanum tuberosum,* made its way, probably from Spain, sometime during the 17th century and soon became a staple. Potatoes grew like magic in the Irish soil and climate, proved attractive to Irish taste, and served beautifully as livestock fodder should wounds or bruises have rendered the tubers unfit for human consumption. The Irish soon learned, like the Incas, to ferment, refine, and enjoy the potato's juices as potent poteen. (This particular discovery has been duplicated by every culture the potato has entered.) Ease of production and storage, combined with enormous harvests, endeared it to the Irish farmer's heart. Even the battles that periodically devastated the land had little effect on the potatoes growing safely underground.

What the English dubbed "the Irish potato" quickly became Eire's mainstay. It was prayed for, sung about, written to, written about, courted with diminutives and fond declarations. Its fields were sprinkled with holy water and blessed each spring to insure good crops. Seed potatoes were ritually planted on Good Friday of each year, since on that date the moon was guaranteed to be on the wane, long an astrological guarantee for successful growing of any underground vegetable. Harvest rites demanded that "first fruits," once mature, be eaten by the whole family as a guarantee of sound storage through the winter. Estimates suggest that by the 19th century everyone in Ireland routinely ate 10 to 12 potatoes daily. The whole economy and the people's diet were bound up in potatoes. No wonder that the Great Potato Blight of 1845-46 was catastrophic. With the bulk of Ireland's potatoes utterly destroyed, over a million people died in the subsequent famine. Thousands emigrated to North America simply to escape sure starvation at home.

The potato had preceded this Irish migration to America by many years, but exactly when or how it got to North America still remains a mystery. It may have travelled along Indian trading routes well before white men even suspected the New World existed. Or it may have come in with the early Spanish or English explorers. In any event, the potato's residence in the Colonies became official in 1719, with the arrival of a group of Scotch-Irish settlers in Londonderry, New Hampshire. These settlers, in gratitude to their favorite crop, erected a monument to it in the town square.

The names of European cultures for the mighty potato are indicative of their sentiments toward it. The French and German names — *pomme de terre* and *Erdapfel,* both of which mean "apple of the earth" — connote both the Garden of Eden and buried treasure. Another German name, also used by Slavic countries, is *Kartoffel,* or truffle, which suggests both a mysterious underground habitat and a sublime flavor. The Irish nicknamed their national vegetable *praties.*

Of the many countries in the world that produce potatoes, Russia and Germany grow the most, followed closely by the United States, where spuds are grown on a commercial basis in every state in the Union. Washington, Oregon, and Maine lead the pack, just ahead of Minnesota's Red River Valley and North Dakota. Because of the range of climatic zones in the country, no month of the year passes without a potato harvest somewhere. Yet the crop sown in the spring and dug in the fall continues to dominate both large- and small-scale operations.

According to government statistics, Americans obtain a higher percentage of carbohydrate requirements from potatoes than from any other source. This is not because the potato is higher in calories and carbohydrate content per se — far from it: an average spud, baked, contains only about 100 calories and 26 grams of carbohydrate, considerably less than an equivalent amount of rice, noodles, or bread. No, it is rather that potatoes are made up of what are called "complex" carbohydrates, starches and fibers that require more effort on the part of the body to digest, and in return furnish the body with more of the substances needed for good health and energy. Between 40% and 60% of the body's daily intake of nourishment should be in the form of these complex carbohydrates, according to nutrition experts.

Actually, carbohydrates are comparatively less fattening than either fats or proteins. All three are necessary for good health, but fats, of which the body needs least, boast almost twice as many calories per gram as the other two; potatoes contain no fat. Add to this caloric economy the fact that each potato contains an astonishing amount and variety of vital nutrients. In fact, nutritionists say that a diet of potatoes and whole milk can furnish everything a normal healthy person needs, so complete is the combined offering.

The overall nutritional content of a potato, including important trace minerals, is impressive indeed. Each potato furnishes significant amounts of vitamin C and several B vitamins — niacin, riboflavin, thiamin, and B_6. Minerals include calcium, phosphorus, iron, sodium, potassium, copper, magnesium, iodine, folic acid, and zinc. Most of these nutritional benefits lie in a thin layer just under the potato's skin. To get the best of the potato, therefore, either do not peel at all and eat the skin along with the rest, or, if peel you must, peel away only the thinnest possible layer of skin. (The recipes in this book are made with unpeeled potatoes unless otherwise specified.)

The average American potato-eater consumes about 120 pounds of spuds each year, but oddly enough, the demand for fresh potatoes in the supermarket is declining. How can we possibly be eating more but buying fewer? The answer is in the ever-increasing amount and variety of processed potatoes being marketed and consumed. Everyone is familiar with the dried granules that make up — poof! — into mashed potatoes in minutes, and with dehydrated potato flakes, slices, and dice. Potatoes also come canned — sliced or small and whole. They come frozen in an endless array of heat-and-eat shapes and forms — from French fries in four designs, to hash browns diced or chunked, to slices for casseroles or stews, to fully prepared, elaborate casseroles.

The range of potato chips alone is staggering. You can buy them salted or unsalted; natural or (presumably) unnatural; flavored with sour cream or onion or both, with chives and barbecue seasonings; sliced thick or thin; peeled or unpeeled; in flat rounds or in shoestrings; made from sliced whole potatoes or stamped from dehydrated granules. Every picnic demands them, every kid adores them. In one form or another, one flavor or another, potato chips are inescapable and ubiquitous.

Oddly enough, this most American food came into being as one man's attempt at vengeance. On a soft summer evening in 1853, at a grand hotel near Saratoga Lake, New York, some finicky guests took exception to the chef's way with potatoes, saying his French fries were too "fat." Chef George

Crum, annoyed by this ridiculous complaint, took a new batch of potatoes and sliced them as thin as he possibly could. These he fried and salted and sent out to the guests, anticipating cries of outrage. Instead he heard "oohs" and "aahs" of content; he had invented a food that would spawn a million-dollar business.

The potato industry today, in all its phases, is big business. New varieties of potato constantly emerge that are more resistant to disease and can better withstand the rigors of mechanical harvesting and processing. New techniques make harvesting and processing more and more efficient.

Although many of the new developments are primarily for the benefit of commercial growers and processors, home gardeners also profit. New strains of potatoes — that produce more tubers per plant, are more disease-resistant, are easier to store, or are more uniformly shaped — can be grown on a small scale just as well as on a large one. Constantly being refined and tailored, the Russet strains are a good example; designed for commercial growers, they are easy to raise in the home garden, resist many diseases, yield well, store well, and can be cooked in every way imaginable.

Restaurants exist today that serve nothing but potatoes — with a wide choice of toppings that turn a plain old spud into a gourmet feast. Potato skins, either freshly freed of their baked contents or peeled raw and fried to crunchy crispness, are the hottest new cocktail nibble since potato chips. Other restaurants feature "potato bars," like the popular salad bars, but starring potatoes. And, yes, there is even a fast-food chain that pushes only potatoes, covered with a miraculously broad array of concoctions.

Potatoes have come a long way from being the secret store of the Incas, locked in the Andean heights of South America. Today, they rank as one of the world's major food crops, and their popularity is still growing.

PLANTING AND CULTIVATION

The taste and texture of potatoes fresh from the potato patch are beyond compare, but many gardeners deny themselves these pleasures because they mistakenly assume that potatoes are just too darned hard to grow. It's not true. In fact, some of the growing methods that use mulch are practically maintenance-free. Potatoes are simply set out in the spring and harvested when ready, protected en route to maturity by heavy mulch.

Even if planted in the earth in the traditional way, potatoes are not complicated to raise. Get the plot ready; balance the soil and make sure water is available; choose the variety of potato right for your conditions; and buy certified seed potatoes. Once the crop is in the ground, keep ahead of bugs and diseases and make water available at a steady rate. If this basic recipe of preparation and maintenance is followed, a bumper crop of firm potatoes is almost sure to be found beneath the soil at harvest time.

Potato Anatomy

The potato is quite a remarkable piece of natural engineering. It is not really the fruit of the potato plant at all, but is instead a cleverly designed underground storehouse, a specialized stem that enlarges on demand as the parent plant stocks it with starch it may need in the future. Until the stem joining the repository and the main plant is broken at harvest-time, the tuber continues to receive and hold this starch.

When the tubers are dug out from the ground, their stem-like features are more apparent. The potato's eyes are dormant true buds, ready on cue to sprout and recreate the parent plant. They are identical in genetic material to the plant. Over these eyes are rudimentary leaf scars called "eyebrows." The fine dots that spatter the potato's skin are its breathing apparatus; they are called lenticels, and correspond exactly to the lenticels found along the plant's true stems. Compare the two — tuber and true stem — and see.

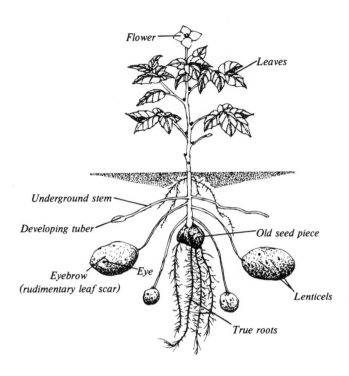

Flower

Leaves

Underground stem

Developing tuber

Old seed piece

Eyebrow
(rudimentary leaf scar)

Eye

Lenticels

True roots

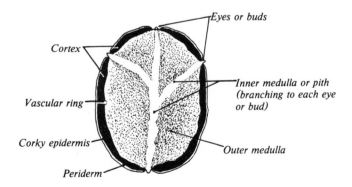

Eyes or buds

Cortex

Vascular ring

Corky epidermis

Periderm

Inner medulla or pith
(branching to each eye
or bud)

Outer medulla

Reproduction

Potatoes bloom and often produce tomato-like fruits, but these flowers and fruits have nothing to do with the formation of tubers underground. The fruits, called "berries," contain seeds that have formed as a result of pollination, and those seeds will grow into potato plants genetically different from either of the parents whose material combined to form the seeds. The potatoes generated by the new plant will also differ from those of the parent plants. Therefore, unless pollination is strictly controlled (as in research into new varieties), using seeds to propagate potato plants is highly unsatisfactory as a means of producing uniform potatoes.

On the other hand, the tubers themselves, used as seed potatoes, inevitably produce exact duplicates of the parent plant, and each duplicate yields the same kind of potato. The eyes on each tuber are the key to accurate regeneration, and the only way known so far to produce a field of plants that will all furnish the same kind of potato.

Were reproduction left entirely to the tubers, and the tubers left in the ground from one year to the next, the potato would be essentially a perennial plant, reproducing itself each spring from tubers of the previous year. But gardeners do not need the enormous number of plants that would result, and do want the tubers, so potatoes are dug each fall and replanted the following spring — a practice which sharply decreases the chance of disease.

Soil Preparation

Potatoes grow best in good sandy loam that is rock free. If your soil is not this ideal type — and most are not — do not despair. Add generous amounts of compost or well-rotted manure to leaven soil that is too sandy or too heavy. These additives also contribute important nutrients, which the potatoes then turn to their own advantage. Pick out rocks during spring plowing or planting and again at harvest time.

Although manure or compost can improve even the best soil, remember that too fresh or too much manure encourages the scab fungus, so do not overdo it. Use only well-rotted manure, at least a year old. Either spread manure on the plot in the fall, or add year-old manure the following spring, working it thoroughly into the soil before planting. Add cow or horse manure at the rate of 2 bushels for each 100 feet of row; add poultry, sheep, goat, or rabbit manure at half that rate.

pH VALUE

Potatoes are very sensitive to acidity, preferring moderately acid soil with pH value between 4.8 and 5.6. In soil sweeter than 5.6, danger of scab infestation increases dramatically. Therefore, avoid liming the soil the same season potatoes are to be planted. Lime a year ahead, preferably, and in any case let at least six months elapse between liming and planting. Plant freshly-limed soil with a crop that appreciates it — legumes or green manures are ideal because they make the soil all that much nicer for the potatoes that are to follow.

Recent scientific findings call into question the value of the traditional practice of adding wood ashes to the potato patch; they may be high in potash, but they also encourage scab. Better not.

Test your soil's pH value with a kit purchased from the hardware or garden supply store. Or ask the county extension agency to send someone out to do it for you. Test soil from several areas of the garden, since conditions can vary radically in a relatively small area. Adjust the soil in response to test results, adding whatever you need for a balanced environment.

If your soil tests too sour — pH below 4.8 — sweeten it by sprinkling lime on top. But be sure to let a full year or at least six months pass before planting potatoes in the limed plot.

If your soil tests on the sweet side — pH about 5.4 or above — reduce the alkalinity by working in ripe manure or compost, or decayed sawdust. In extreme cases, add judicious amounts of aluminum sulfate or ammonium sulfate to the soil, carefully following package directions. If you add sawdust, be sure to add extra nitrogen fertilizer with it because decaying sawdust will leach existing nitrogen from the soil.

THE PLOT

The area where potatoes grow should be well-drained, since soggy soil spawns rot and assorted other problems. Potatoes are a hardy crop and can survive mild drought conditions, but they will suffer some ill effects. When they lack sufficient water, they wisely suspend growth, resuming when moisture again becomes available. This stop-and-go growing will cause the tubers to become knobby, lumpy, or hollow-hearted. For good steady growth, potatoes need water at the rate of about one inch per week on a regular basis. If normal rainfall does not supply this amount, water the patch yourself thoroughly — until the soil is moist to a depth of 10 to 12 inches. Do this weekly during dry spells.

Do not plant potatoes in the same spot in successive years, or in an area where tomatoes, peppers, eggplants, petunias, strawberries, or brambles were grown the previous year. All these plants share susceptibility to a wide range of viruses and funguses that lurk in the soil. It is best to let two full seasons pass between such plantings. Use the years between to enrich the soil with a legume crop that fixes nitrogen and a green manure crop that adds organic matter. Or plant a crop with different nutritional requirements, such as squash, corn, or coles. By the third year, any harmful organisms should have subsided, and potatoes and/or their cousins should be in no danger. Followed regularly, this rotation schedule will benefit all your garden crops.

If your garden is already chock-full of other vegetables, plant small amounts of potatoes in flower beds, along borders, or in containers. Potato foliage and flowers are as pretty as can be, and accent their surroundings very nicely.

FERTILIZER

If you are the kind of gardener who uses chemical fertilizer to help things along, either 10-10-10 or 5-10-5 worked into rows or hills at planting time will take potatoes right through the season. Apply fertilizer in moderation; in this case more is not necessarily better, since too much potassium or nitrogen in the soil engenders rot.

Alternatives to chemical fertilizers are particularly suited to growing potatoes. Potassium from granite dust or greensand (ocean sand); nitrogen from legumes, green manures, blood meal, cottonseed meal, fish emulsion, or animal manures; phosphorous from bone meal or phosphate rock; and a host of nutrients and trace minerals from ripe compost or manure set the stage for a bountiful crop.

Use a soil-testing kit or advice from the county extension agent to guide you in balancing the nutritional content of your soil.

Amount to Grow

Growing enough potatoes to sustain an entire family for the winter takes a lot of doing, and a lot of land. Because the average family consumes 10 to 20 bushels each winter, the average garden is rarely up to this amount, although an average gardener *can* produce a good part of the winter's potato supply, and be mighty proud of the results.

In general, 10 pounds of seed potatoes will seed about 100 feet of row, which will usually produce between one and two bushels of potatoes (six to eight pounds per plant). Why not buy small amounts of several different varieties and plant them all? That way you will have the fun of sampling tastes and types not generally available in the grocery stores, and of eating them freshly dug as they ripen. Any extras can be stored for use in the winter to liven up the store-bought kinds.

Choosing Seed

Choose the variety of potato that will do best in your soil and climate. This is the most important aspect of the selection process, if you truly want to end the season with a successful crop.

Numerous varieties are available to the home gardener (see list of varieties and sources where they can be purchased, pp. 47-50). These are classified by shape, skin type, texture, ability to resist diseases, and date of maturity — early, mid-season, or late. Growing time varies with each strain of

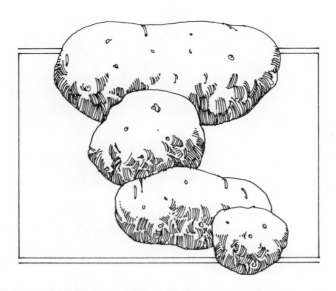

Potato Shapes. *From top to bottom:* (a) — *long, with "white" or russet skin;* (b) — *round, with "white" or red skin;* (c) & (d) — *new potatoes, with "white," red, or russet skin.*

potato. The range is from 90 days for early types to 105 days for late kinds. Keep the specific requirements of your chosen varieties in mind as you decide when to plant.

Most strains grow best when nights are on the cool side, below 70°F., and days stay below 80°F., but modern research has produced potatoes that grow well under higher temperatures. Even so, southern gardeners should choose carefully; varieties with short growing seasons do best, since they ripen before the real heat of summer sets in. If specific diseases, such as verticillium wilt or mosaic, are a problem in your area, select varieties bred to resist the organisms that cause these diseases. Available, for example, are strains that resist assorted rots, mosaic viruses of several different types, and even some physiological defects. Know what problems you are apt to encounter and try to avoid them.

In any case, always buy seed potatoes that are certified disease-free. This is very important if long-term problems with viral and fungal organisms are to be averted. Supermarket potatoes will grow, unless treated not to, and so will uncertified seed potatoes, but chances are high that they will carry diseases that can make the plot unusable for several years.

Above all, when you select potatoes to grow, keep in mind their eventual use. Some varieties are best for boiling, others for baking; some don't store well, others keep almost indefinitely. Plant varieties that keep well if you plan to store any at all.

Seed Potatoes

When buying certified seed potatoes for planting, look for the smaller "B" size; these are usually available at the local garden supply outlet, if not through mail order. Because they are small, "B" size potatoes can be planted whole and thus eliminate one more chance of infection. The wounds on seed potatoes cut into sowing-size pieces, if not properly suberized, provide an ideal avenue for germs to enter and get to work. (Suberizing is the healing process that toughens the flesh where the cut was made.)

Five or six weeks ahead of planting time, take whole seed potatoes and spread them in a single layer in a place with bright diffused light. The temperature should be about 60°F. Allow the potatoes to "green," turning them frequently so that all sides become equally green and sprouts appear from the eyes. Discard weak or spindly sprouts and any sickly potatoes. "Greening" speeds early growth and helps you distinguish the stronger sprouts. Then, cut large potatoes into planting pieces, each about the size of a chicken's egg and including at least one healthy eye or strong sprout. Dust the pieces with fungicide formulated to combat soil-borne problems, available at garden-supply stores (this treatment speeds suberizing), and let the pieces suberize for three or four days at about 70°F.

Seed potatoes ordered through the mail do not always come small enough to plant without cutting, but the catalog will tell you whether your seed potatoes are sent whole, or in pieces ("B" size seed potatoes need not be cut). If they have been cut up at the supply house, the pieces will have already been treated against potential infection.

Plant early potatoes five or six weeks before the date of

the last expected frost in your area, or as soon as the ground can be worked. Southern gardeners can plant in January or February. The young plants take some time to break through the soil, and are quite able to withstand the last few frosts of spring once they do emerge.

Plant mid-season potatoes at just about the time of the last frost of spring.

Calculate when to plant late potatoes by counting backwards from the date of the first hard frost of fall back toward summer the number of days given for their growing season, and plant accordingly. Planting is best timed so that the potatoes will be diggable two or three weeks ahead of the first really severe frost, although two or three weeks on either side of that date will still work.

While underground, potatoes will not be touched by the first frosts, since the soil will insulate them. The frost will kill off the plants, however, if old age has not already done so. Late potatoes, by and large, are the best kinds to store, since they tend to keep for longer stretches of time without rotting or sprouting.

Germination

Do not be alarmed if sprouts take a while to emerge in your garden. Shoots take from 8 to 16 days to break through the soil, and cold weather can delay them further.

Planting

The potato gardener wants to provide his plants with the perfect underground environment. It is here that the potatoes form as enlargements on the stems used to store nourishment as starch. The assortment of planting methods outlined below takes advantage of this environment in a variety of ways, some requiring more of the gardener than others, but all aimed at producing lots of nice big potatoes.

There are four basic ways to plant potatoes, each of which has its own particular virtues. The four methods are: planting in rows, planting in hills, planting under mulch, and planting in containers for ornamental purposes. An outline of each follows.

ROW METHOD

This is probably the most common, although not necessarily the easiest. It is certainly characteristic of any commercial potato-raising operation, and often of home gardens as well.

Once seed potatoes are ready for planting and the soil is ready to receive them, make a series of trenches, each 6 inches deep and 24 to 36 inches from the next. Place seed potatoes or potato pieces (cut sides down) in the trenches, 12 to 18 inches apart along the trench, *except* for larger potatoes such as Russet varieties. Seeds or pieces of large-tubered varieties should be planted only 6 to 12 inches apart to prevent

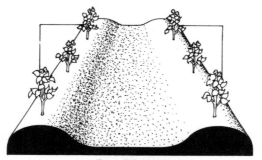

Row Method.

over-rapid growth. If the tubers grow too fast, the middle will become hollow and coarse — a condition known as "hollow heart." Cover the potatoes with two to four inches of dirt, leaving the remaining loose soil piled alongside each trench. A soil cover of two inches allows the young shoots to break through sooner, and may reduce chances of rhizoctonia and blackleg disease (see pp. 39 and 40). A four-inch cover gives extra protection from late frosts.

When the young plants have emerged and have grown to about nine inches in height, mound some of the reserved soil from the trench around them, leaving only six inches exposed. Repeat this process once every three weeks from this time until the plants blossom, gradually using up the loose dirt and ending with a trench full of soil and potatoes. This mounding process is necessary to good potato production, since it protects the developing potatoes from the deleterious effects of the sun.

During the growing season, keep weeds down along and between the rows. Wield the hoe or rake very carefully, disturbing only the top two inches of soil; deeper cultivation is apt to sever the links between the plant and its potatoes.

HILL METHOD

Although similar to the row method, this requires less space, and the plants are easier to tend during the growing season.

To plant in hills, dig holes two or three inches deep, spacing them 12 to 18 inches apart in all directions (again except for large tubered potatoes, which should be planted only 6 to 12 inches apart). Place a whole potato or a piece in each hole and cover with four inches of soil. When plants are six to nine inches tall, mound the surrounding earth up around the stem

Hill Method.

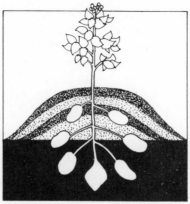

"Hilling Up:" *stripes show successive soil layers piled around growing plant.*

of each plant for about a foot on all sides. This mounding process produces the hill and is repeated every three weeks or so until the plants blossom.

Cultivate weekly, again being careful not to disturb the developing potatoes.

MULCH METHOD

The mulch method is the most care-free way to raise potatoes, provided conditions do not become too wet. Heavy mulching combined with excessive moisture favors an abundance of slugs, not to mention a high incidence of fungus diseases. However, if the potato patch is set in a well-drained area, mulch works beautifully. Potatoes are planted under mulch generally in one of three ways: placed in a six-inch trench dug into the soil and then covered with mulch; placed on top of plowed (or unplowed) ground and piled high with mulch; or placed on top of a thick layer of well-decomposed mulch, instead of on bare ground, and then covered with a second layer of fresh mulch. Use last year's upper mulch for this year's lower layer, or compost the leaves raked in the fall and use them for the lower layer in the spring. In this third variant, the potatoes develop between the old and new layers. Roots sink through the bottom layer; plants emerge through the top.

The main advantages of mulching by any one of these three patterns are the minimal care the plants require during growing season, and the extreme ease of harvesting at the end of the season. All the gardener needs to do during the growing period is simply make sure the mulch around the plants is thick enough (six to eight inches) to protect the tubers from sunlight, and, of course, patrol frequently to defend against marauding insects. At harvest time, the crop is picked by pulling off the top mulch and lifting the waiting potatoes out of the soil or off the ground. No digging, no bruising, no accidental wounding.

Pile mulch good and high around plants, making sure it is six inches to eight inches thick. Either apply it at planting time, or wait and pile it around the young plants when they are about six inches tall.

For mulch over and around plants, use straw, grass cuttings, bark, rotted hay, or leaves. The same set of materials, well on their way to disintegration, provides a good bed if potatoes are to be grown between layers.

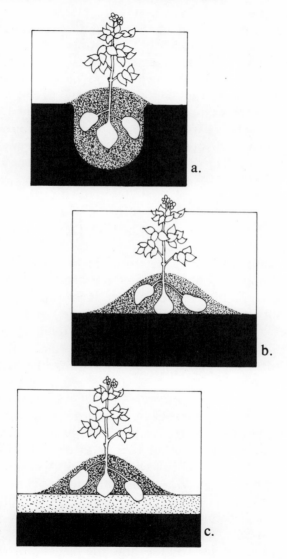

Mulch Methods: (a) — *seed potato placed in trench, then covered with mulch;* (b) — *seed piece placed on top of soil, then covered with mulch;* (c) — *seed piece laid on old mulch and covered with fresh mulch.*

Mulch promotes strong healthy growth in the plants it is protecting. By smothering weeds, mulch relieves the plants of the need to compete for nutrients, and removes the possibility of injury to developing tubers during cultivation. It also holds moisture in the soil, thereby giving the plants a more consistent supply. It protects the underground environment from the sun and keeps the soil cool. This moist, weedless, dark, cool situation is what potatoes like best, and they tend to flourish when properly mulched. Moreover, this season's top mulch, plowed into the soil, will rapidly decompose and nourish next year's crop.

Mulch can also be used in conjunction with the row or hill method. Pile mulch material six to eight inches high along rows or around hills to derive a number of the benefits listed above.

CONTAINER METHOD

If you lack space for a potato patch but crave just a few homegrown spuds, or if an ornamental planting is your aim, you can grow potatoes in a container such as a large garbage can, an empty oil drum, an old potato barrel, or even a stack of three or four old tires. Whatever container you select, make sure it has holes in the bottom for drainage. If they are not already there, poke them. Potatoes sitting in a barrelful of water will do nothing but rot.

In the bottom of the container, put six inches of good sandy loam, with some fertilizer, compost, or manure mixed well into it. On this mixture lay two or three seed potatoes or pieces and cover with another two or three inches of sandy loam. Put the container in full sun. The seeds will soon sprout and the plants emerge. When they are nine inches tall, add another layer of soil, filling the container so that only six inches of plant are visible. Repeat this layering process every 10 days to two weeks, keeping all but the top six inches of the plants covered with soil. By the time the plants stop their upward progress and begin to blossom, the container should be pretty well filled, with the plants peeking over the top.

Give the growing plants plenty of water. They need about

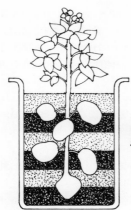

Container Method: *stripes show successive soil layers added as plant grows.*

an inch of water each week; if natural rainfall does not provide it, furnish it for them.

Container-grown potatoes are ready to harvest when the plants turn yellow and die. Once this has happened, either gently remove the soil layer by layer, lifting out the potatoes as you go; or up-end the entire container, dump out its contents, and gently separate the potatoes from the soil. You should be astonished at the number of tubers hidden in the container — usually a bushel or more!

If you are using stacked tires, begin the process with one tire. Fill it with soil, lay the seed pieces on that layer, and cover with another two-or three-inch layer. Add tires and soil as necessary to keep the plants adequately covered as they grow. Water as necessary, of course. Plants grown from tire to tire are assured of receiving ample sunlight, and should flourish. At harvest time, reverse the building process, removing the tires and their contents one by one.

PESTS AND DISEASES

Sad to say, potatoes are the favorite food not only of many people, but also of numerous insects and microbes. Forewarned is definitely forearmed; be aware of threats likely to test your crop, and be ready to defend against them. Many a gardener has taken measures from the start of the season and ended with a perfect crop, while his less alert neighbor has seen his plants and crop eaten up before he knew what was happening. In growing potatoes, an ounce of prevention seems worth several pounds of cure.

Soil-borne diseases pose the most insidious threat to a healthy potato crop. We have already mentioned the importance of planting only certified disease-free seed potatoes and of regular crop rotation (see p. 29 and p. 27).

Among funguses that attack potatoes, early blight and late blight pose the greatest danger. (Late blight was the cause of the Great Irish Potato Famine of 1845-46.) Prevention is the best defense, since once these two funguses get into the patch it is just about impossible to eradicate them.

Scab, another fungus, also strikes at potatoes from the soil and also must be prevented rather than cured. The fungus causes scab-like deformities on the skins of the tubers, and rot during storage.

General Prevention

To prevent these and other diseases (see below), follow these general rules:

1. Consult your county extension agent to find out what funguses are locally prevalent.

2. Choose potato varieties that are bred for specific resistance to such microbes, and plant only certified disease-free stock.

3. Follow recommended practices for soil preparation, planting, and cultivation.

4. Rotate crops regularly, whether specific diseases are locally rampant or not, for the good of the soil and all crops grown there.

5. Maintain healthy soil composition and pH, avoiding fresh manure and fresh lime assiduously.

6. Obtain and use regularly a recommended fungicide (every 7 to 10 days).

Diseases

Here is a list of diseases you may encounter and what to do about them.

Bacterial Soft Rot: caused by the bacterium *Erwinia carotovora;* affects tubers, and is spread through contaminated soil and seed. Tubers first look swollen, with brown soggy spots near any wounds, then dried out. Prevent or control by avoiding infected soil.

Blackleg: caused by the bacterium *Erwinia atroseptica;* affects tubers, and is spread through seed and soil. Signs are tubers rotting from stem ends, with stems themselves black and shiny; sometimes the plant collapses. Prevent by using disease-free seed pieces, and by being careful not to wound tubers.

Dry Rot: caused by *Fusarium* species of fungus; affects tubers, showing brownish areas that dry out and leave cavities and/or sunken areas around lenticels. Prevent by avoiding wounds at harvest time, and letting potatoes "cure" before storage.

Early Blight: caused by the fungus *Alternaria solani* that attacks vines and tubers; spread by soil and seed. Symptoms are tubers with purplish sunken areas defined by raised ring, yellowish flesh, or yellowed or moldy leaves, often showing dark, round or target-like wounds, and vines that seem on the verge of collapse. Prevent by use of fungicides, and by observance of rotation schedules.

Hollow Heart: a physiological disorder caused by improper spacing of plants, and irregular moisture supply. Prevent by planting resistant varieties and observing recommendations for spacing and watering.

Late Blight: caused by the fungus *Phytophohora infestans* that attacks vines and tubers; spreads via air, water, seed pieces, often from infected compost piles nearby. Signs are soggy or puffy tubers with deep, dark-colored lesions; shiny-looking and eventually moldy yellowish leaves. Avoid by destroying unwanted potatoes rather than throwing them into compost heap, by spraying plants with fungicides, by using disease-free seed and resistant varieties, and by killing foliage two weeks before harvesting potatoes.

Leak: caused by the fungus *Pythium debaryanum;* affects tubers. Fungus invades tuber via wound, then causes brown soggy spots, swollen tubers, yellowed interior, eventual drying and oozing. Prevent by planting where drainage is good and by harvesting carefully.

Leaf Roll: a viral disease that attacks vines and tubers. Also called "net necrosis," it is passed along by aphids and infected seed pieces. Leaves roll, shrivel, and die; tubers slowly disintegrate. Prevent by planting disease-free seed of resistant varieties. Watch for diseased plants; pull and destroy them. Control aphids.

Rhizoctonia (Black Scurf): caused by the fungus *Rhizoctonia solani;* hits stems, tubers, and roots, and spreads by way of soil and seed pieces. Potatoes are covered with black spots; stems and roots show reddish lesions, cracks, and darkening. Avoid by planting when soil has become warm, and use disease-free seed.

Ring Rot: caused by the bacterium *Corynebacterium sepedonicum;* affects vines and tubers. Signs are yellowing of stem connecting tuber and plant, eventual separation of stem from tuber, yellow ooze from tuber when squeezed. Plants show stunted growth, wilting, yellowed leaves, oozy stems. Prevent by planting disease-free seed, whole instead of in pieces.

Common Scab: caused by the fungus *Streptomyces scabies;* affects tubers, showing dark, rough, spongy spots. Spreads through soil, so avoid infested areas, rotate crops, plant resistant varieties, control pH level carefully, maintain good drainage.

Silver Scurf: caused by the fungus *Helminthosporium solani;* tubers show mottled skins, red-skinned potatoes have silvery splotches. Plant disease-free seed, rotate crops, grow resistant varieties.

Verticillium Wilt: caused by the *Verticillium* funguses; affects both vines and tubers, and is spread by soil, seed pieces, compost piles. Signs are abnormal tuber formation, collapse and death of vines. Prevent by planting resistant varieties, observing long periods in rotation, planting disease-free seed, destroying diseased potatoes and other solani.

Pests

Lots of different kinds of pests dote on potato plants, but all are fairly easy to discourage with regular attention.

The **Colorado potato beetle** is the worst and most infamous of the bugs that crave potato plants. This rascal has been around for a good many years by now, and arrives each summer in eager hungry hordes, apparently out of the blue. Often it is accompanied by the **flea beetle,** its voracious cousin, much smaller and harder to spot.

Colorado potato beetles are a light tan or gold, with black-striped backs. About an inch long, the beetles appear in the spring and lay clusters of bright orange eggs on the undersides of leaves. Both the beetles themselves and the fat, black-spotted, red grubs that hatch from the eggs dine non-stop on potato leaves.

The **Mexican bean beetle** is the third in this trio of foliage-feasters. The primary target of these beetles is beans, but they settle quite happily for potatoes if beans are unavailable. Adults are about ¾ inch long, red with black spots. The eggs are yellow, the insatiable larvae also yellow and somewhat fuzzy.

Aphids too like potatoes and can seriously harm a crop by sucking sap from leaves and stems. Less than ⅛ inch long, aphids come in a variety of colors — black, grey, brown, yellow, red, lavender, green. Prime culprits in the spread of virus diseases, they can be spotted by the accumulation of "honeydew," droplets of excretion, which itself promotes sooty mold.

Leafhoppers resemble tiny grasshoppers. They hop from leaf to leaf, congregating in groups on the underside to suck the sap. Foliage attacked by leafhoppers turns yellow or brown and dies. These nuisances also carry several viruses which can further damage the crop.

Pests which dwell not on the plants themselves but in the soil around them include **white grubs, wireworms,** and **cutworms.**

The first two are most common in soil just converted to garden from sod. Avoid them by letting a full year elapse between the time the garden is dug and the time you plant any crop in the soil.

Cutworms, on the other hand, are almost always around. They come out at night in spring when young plants are most vulnerable, and eat through the stems at ground level. During the day the worms, which come in several sizes and colors, retreat beneath the soil. They can be foiled easily enough. As soon as young shoots emerge from the soil, encircle them with a collar of cardboard, plastic, or metal three inches wide. Put the collar around the young plant stem and press it into the soil about an inch, leaving two inches above ground. Cutworms cannot breach this simple barricade.

In combating pests, you can, of course, use chemicals. Follow the recommendations of your county extension agent or local garden supply store. Use chemical pesticides strictly according to directions. But remember that anything you apply to your potato plants or the soil around them eventually ends up in the tubers and thence inside the bodies of the tuber-eaters. Several entirely natural deterrents exist, especially with regard to potato beetles, flea beetles, leafhoppers, and aphids, that leave no chemical residue.

Easiest of these is simple intercropping — planting a crop repellent (or more attractive) to the insects that like the potato patch. Beans are the best known counter to potato pests (except, of course, bean beetles), but horseradish, corn, cabbage, marigolds, limas, and flax will serve as well. Eggplant, prey to the same pests, is used by some gardeners to protect their potato crop. Evidently, the only thing tastier than a potato to a hungry beetle is a sacrificial eggplant. Thus beetles devour the eggplant and leave the potatoes unmolested. Members of the cucurbit (squash) family planted among early potatoes serve two purposes: first, they discourage beetles; then later, when the early potato crops are done, the ebullient squashes move into the space left open.

A third alternative, and one that seems almost too good to be true, albeit a trifle ghoulish, entails application of a spray prepared from the pests themselves. Opinion differs as to the reason for its effectiveness — a pathogen released by the spray; an odor that attracts predators to consume the pest in question; or distress pheromones that signal to others of the pest species that this way lies danger. Suffice it that the spray is highly effective, and is easily tailored to the specific problem. To make a batch of spray, collect a good handful of the pests that are doing the damage. Put the insects in the blender with two cups of water and blend for about a minute, until the substance is thoroughly pureed. Strain the puree through cheesecloth (otherwise it may clog the sprayer). Then fill the sprayer with puree and water in the ratio of one part puree to four parts water (e.g. one-quarter cup puree and one cup water) and spray potato plants liberally, dousing the undersides of leaves and up and down the stems as well as the tops of leaves.

Other remedies are more laborious: picking beetles, larvae, and eggs off by hand and dropping them into detergent or kerosene, for example.

When slugs are a problem (especially during wet weather), collect them under pieces of cantaloupe skin or grapefruit peel, then scoop up and destroy. The potato itself, used as a lure for several pests, also works against slugs. Thick slices of mature potato (not necessarily the variety being grown), laid out in the patch at frequent intervals, attract many common pests. Collect used slices with their bountiful aggregations frequently, and replace with fresh slices. Slugs, snails, cutworms, and grubs all find such slices more alluring than the sap and adolescent flesh of potatoes still on the vine.

Rather than a separate antidote for each pest, some gardeners prefer a general concoction that will repel just about everything. One recipe for a homemade repellent is as follows: Brew a tea of boiling water and 1 tablespoon wormwood, 1 teaspoon garlic, 2 tablespoons chives, 1 teaspoon hot pepper, and 2 tablespoons mint. Strain the tea and dilute it with 4 parts water. Spray infested plants liberally, coating tops and bottoms of leaves and stems. If spray doesn't want to stick, add a teaspoon of detergent to it. This spray applied to potatoes and other plants deters insects of all sorts.

So, in brief, be alert for signs of serious wilting, progressive yellowing, devastated foliage, or abundant insects — all are calls to action.

Start off on the right foot by planting potatoes with a second species that discourages pests — beans or whatever. If this is not sufficient deterrent, try the other measures recommended. Should you decide to resort to commercial sprays, make sure you use one that is approved by the USDA, and follow directions for its use very carefully.

HARVEST

It surprises many gardeners to learn that potatoes need not be harvested all at once. Part or all of the tubers on any one plant can be picked from blossom-time on. Potatoes harvested before full maturity are called "new" potatoes, and are extra tender and tasty. Extract them gently and carefully from the soil beneath their mother plant, being absolutely sure not to disturb any potatoes not being dug. New potatoes justify harvesting from the time they are at least one inch in diameter. Remove them by hand at this early stage; if the stems joining other tubers are disturbed, the tubers will cease to grow and start to rot. If you are growing potatoes under mulch and want to sample them before full maturity, all you need to do is gently peel back the mulch, lift out the potatoes you want, and then replace the covering so the rest can keep on growing.

The main potato harvest comes later, when plants and tubers have grown to maturity. Now comes the best moment of all, the time when the gardener reaps the reward for his season-long dedication to his unseen treasure.

The potatoes are ready when the tops of the plants turn yellow, wilt, and die. Once this stage is reached, the tubers will be safe in the ground for another two weeks or so, even if the first few frosts fall during this period. The soil protects them from frostbite, and this two-week grace period gives them time to develop tougher skins that present greater resistance to bruising or rot during storage. However, if the first frosts arrive before the plants have died on their own, go through the patch and lop them off the vines at soil level; then let the tubers rest for 10 to 14 days undisturbed underground to toughen up. Test potatoes for harvest readiness by pushing the skin with a thumb. If the skin does not give, the potatoes can come out.

Although potatoes generally benefit from a couple of extra weeks in the ground after maturity, if at any time during this period the weather suddenly becomes warm and/or wet, remove them promptly. Unseasonal conditions promote rot and unhealthy renewed growth; either can wreck a perfect crop.

When you dig the potatoes, do it when the ground and the weather are fairly dry. Use a spading fork (or narrow-tined pitchfork for mulch-grown potatoes) to bring them forth. Begin to turn up the soil with its load of potatoes about 18 inches out from the center of the plant, and work inward. Dig down deeply, and gently shake the forkfuls as you lift them out so that tubers and soil will separate. Leave the potatoes, still encrusted with whatever earth clings to them, on top of the ground to cure for one or two hours, then gather and store them. Do not leave them out longer, because the skins, accustomed only to darkness, will suffer burn or scald from wind or sun. In addition, potatoes are still prone to develop solanin toxin even at this mature stage, turning bitter and green in response to excess sun.

When digging and collecting potatoes, try not to bruise or puncture them. Wounds of any kind inflicted on them at this stage create opportunities for bugs and bacteria, viruses and funguses to invade and commence eating the flesh.

STORAGE

Once dug and cured, potatoes are ready for eating or storage. If they are to be stored, do not wash them. Store them unwashed, in the dark, in a room where the temperature stays constantly between 35° and 50°F. (2° to 4°C.), and the humidity averages 85% to 90%. The room must also have ventilation so that gases produced by the transpiration of the stored potatoes can be vented to the outside and replaced with fresh air, and so the chill outside air of winter can help keep the storage area cool. Store the potatoes in wooden boxes or bins about 18 inches deep, or shallower, so that air can circulate freely among the tubers. Barring scab, or rot due to bruising or wounding at harvest, stored potatoes should keep for as long as eight months.

Chances that potatoes will sprout and shrivel increase in temperatures above about 40°F. and increase radically at temperatures over 50°F. Should your storage area fail to provide the proper temperature, a substance that inhibits sprouting is available at garden-supply stores. This substance is applied to the whole plant during the growing season. It is taken in through the leaves and passed along to the tubers, where it is stored, coming into action during the winter when sprouting threatens. Most potatoes sold in stores have been treated with a sprout-inhibitor, especially potatoes that appear on the shelves after early January. Early spring, after all, is the time when plants begin to grow again, and uninhibited potatoes sprout enthusiastically.

Store potatoes in the dark. During storage as during growing and harvest, exposure to light induces solanin greening, which makes the potatoes bitter and slightly poisonous. Discard any potatoes that show signs of this condition.

If the temperature of your storage chamber slips below about 35°F., and especially if it drops below freezing, you will find that your potatoes taste strangely sweet. The starch for which they are so famous has, in fact, been converted to sugar by the cold. The resulting sweet taste is not particularly pleasant, but the damage is easily reversed. Sugar reconverts to starch if the affected potatoes are kept at a temperature of about 70°F. for a week — in the dark of course. The potato will gradually resume its starchy taste. Once the situation has righted itself, return the potatoes to the storage area, this time making sure the temperature stays between 35° and 50°F.

Should harvest time and serious frosts arrive before your potato cellar is ready, you still have two or three weeks grace period between the time of digging the potatoes and the time they absolutely must be stored as prescribed above. Entirely dormant during this interval, the tubers can be stored pretty much anywhere, as long as they are in *the dark*. But grace period is *all* it is — potatoes should be put into the proper environment — cool, moist, ventilated, and dark — as soon as possible.

VARIETIES

ALL BLUE (Gurney): Novelty potato with blue flesh and blue skin. Bakes, boils, and fries well and has a good flavor. Makes a grand Fourth of July salad when combined with white potatoes and pimiento or beets.

ANOKA (Gurney): An older variety best for frying or boiling. Has round shape, smooth skin, matures early.

BAKE KING (Gurney): Gurney claims the best baking potato of all because of its extra-mealy texture. Bakes well whole or sliced and done up in casseroles. Has white skin with slight russeting, oblong shape, shallow eyes. Produces high yields and resists defects like hollow heart. Blooms white, matures mid-season.

BLUE VICTOR (Gurney): An old favorite among novelty-growers, but now becoming scarce. Has flattish oblong shape, is medium in size. High specific gravity makes it good for boiling. White flesh, blue skin.

CHIPPEWA (Olds): Long tubers with pale skin, white flesh. Yields very well, especially in northern regions. Bakes or boils with aplomb. Used by the potato chip industry because it holds its shape and texture when cooked. Blossoms are pale lilac. Ripens mid-season.

COBBLER (May, Burpee, Field): Home gardeners' favorite because of flavor, texture, early maturity. Great for baking but stores less well than Kennebec or Red Pontiac. Bears lilac flowers. Matures early.

EARLY GEM (Olds): U.S. potato most resistant to early scab. Tubers longish, with shallow eyes and rough skin. Ready early.

EARLY OHIO (Farmer): Standard round potato. Good boiled or fried. Older variety. Matures early.

FINGERLINGS (Olds): Brought from Germany by early settlers — their favorite salad potato. Has yellow flesh, produces long narrow tubers with excellent flavor. Best boiled unpeeled and sliced for salad.

GERMAN PURPLE (Olds): Another originally German variety — little round tubers with purple skin and yellow flesh, generally about 1½ inches in diameter. Boil and slice unpeeled for salad.

IRISH COBBLER (Farmer, Meyer): Direct ancestor of White Cobbler, and largely supplanted by it. Old favorite with round shape, white flesh, smooth thin skin, deep eyes. Excellent boiled. Blossoms are lilac. Ready early.

KATAHDIN (Meyer): Former mainstay of Maine's potato crop, but now less popular. Good for boiling or frying. Comes round, with pale skin, white flesh, medium size or larger. Yields well, resists mild mosaic, net necrosis, virus Y, leafroll. Flowers are lilac and white. Matures late.

KENNEBEC (Burpee, Farmer, Field, Gurney, Lakeland, May, Meyer, Olds): Very resistant to blight and mosaic. Tubers long, with white flesh and skin. Grows well on most soils, keeps well in storage; but needs protection from sun because highly susceptible to sun-greening and solanin buildup. Fertilize in moderation to prevent over-developed lumpy tubers. Flowers are white, maturity is mid-season.

LADY FINGER (Gurney): Gurney's name for Fingerling. See description above.

MAYFAIR (May): Large oblong tubers with russeted skin, white flesh, and shallow eyes. Excellent for all uses — baking, boiling, frying, salad. Yields well. Matures mid-season.

NORCHIP (Gurney): Offered as a replacement for White Cobbler. Yields well, resistant to flea beetle, scab, and silver scurf, but tends to sprout in storage. Blossoms are white, maturity is early.

NORGOLD RUSSET (Farmer, Field, Gurney, Olds): Has long shape, smooth netted skin, white flesh. Boils and bakes well; resists scab. Plant only 6"-12" apart to avoid "hollow heart" and outsize tubers. Produces pink flowers; matures early.

NORLAND (Gurney, Farmer, Field, May, Meyer, Olds): Gurney calls theirs "New Norland," but varieties are essentially the same. Round potatoes with smooth red skin, shallow eyes, and very white flesh. Plants are somewhat scab resistant, but easily succumb to other diseases. Tubers boil and bake very well. Purple flowers emerge early; matures early also.

RED LA SODA (Olds): Yields well in wide range of soils and climates, so makes an excellent choice for the home gardener. Has red skin, round shape, firm flesh. Good boiled or mashed. Blossoms are purple. Maturity is early to mid-season.

RED McCLURE (Park): A traditional all-purpose potato, round in shape with thin red skin. Matures early.

RED PONTIAC (Burpee, Farmer, Field, Gurney, Lakeland, May, Meyer, Olds): Tubers are large, round, red-skinned with white flesh. Plants yield well on almost all soils. Tubers store well, but handle carefully, because they bruise easily and then go bad. Good boiled or in salad. Flowers are light mauve, tipped with white. Maturity is mid-season.

RUSSET BURBANK (Field, Park, Olds): The most familiar potato. Long shape, thicker brown skin. Variety resists scab, likes constant, moderate water supply. Tubers keep well. Best for baking. Flowers are white, tubers mature late.

RUSSET SEBAGO (Olds): A tougher-skinned Sebago that resists scab and late blight. Flowers are maroon. Yields well. Oblong tubers with white flesh; matures late.

SEBAGO (Olds): Skin is pale and thin, shape is oval, flesh is white. Plants resist late blight and stand up to assaults of potato leafhoppers. Also shrugs off Yellow Dwarf disease. Yields well, but susceptible to scab. A paradox, since plants do best in fertile soil that encourages scab. Be careful. Grows best where weather is hotter — Florida, southern states. Flowers are lilac, maturity late.

SUPERIOR (Farmer, Meyer, Olds): Oval shape, thin brown skin, white flesh, deepish eyes. All-purpose potato. Lavender flowers, early maturity.

VIKING (May): Large potatoes, round and red-skinned. Yield is high and crop stores well. Tubers good for all uses. Matures early to mid-season. A good dependable variety.

SOURCES

(Catalogs are available on request.)

Burpee Seed Co.
Warminster, PA 18991

Eyes from certified disease-free potatoes. Kennebec, Red Pontiac, White Cobbler.

Farmer Seed and Nursery Co.
Faribault, Minnesota 55021

Eyes from certified seed potatoes. Norgold Russet, Norland, Kennebec, Superior Red Pontiac.

Gurney Seed & Nursery Co.
Yankton, SD 57079

Eyes from certified seed potatoes. New Norland, Norchip, Kennebec, Anoka, Red Pontiac, Norgold Russet, Bake King, Lady Finger, Blue Victor, All Blue.

Lakeland Nurseries
Hanover, PA 17331

Eyes from certified seed potatoes. Red Pontiac, Kennebec; also sets for "Tompato" plants, where tomatoes grow above and potatoes grow below ground. Further refinement offers tomatoes, potatoes, and peppers from the same plant.

Earl May Seed & Nursery Co.
Shenandoah, Iowa 51603

Eyes from "fresh, clean, solid Northern Grown Seed Potatoes." Red Pontiac, Cobbler, Mayfair, Norland, Kennebec, Viking.

The Meyer Seed Co.
600 South Caroline St.
Baltimore, MD 21231

Whole certified seed potatoes. Irish Cobbler, Katahdin, Kennebec, Norland, Red Pontiac, Superior.

L.L. Olds Seed Co.
P.O. Box 7790
2901 Packers Ave.
Madison, WI 53707

Whole certified seed potatoes. Norgold Russet, Superior, Norland, Early Gem, Red Pontiac, Kennebec, Chippewa, Red La Soda, Sebago, Russet Sebago, Russet Burbank, Fingerlings, German Purple.

Geo. W. Park Seed Co., Inc.
Greenwood, SC 29647

Whole certified seed potatoes. Red McClure, Russet Burbank.

Henry Field Seed & Nursery Co.
407 Sycamore
Shenandoah, IA 51602

Eyes from certified seed potatoes. Kennebec, Norland, Norgold Russet, Red Pontiac, Russet Burbank, White Cobbler.

COOKING POTATOES

BASIC COOKING METHODS

Please read this section before proceeding to the individual recipes. In it you will find directions for boiling, steaming, baking, and frying potatoes to best advantage and to suit your family's taste. Here too are included Kitchen Tips for Potatoes, a whole list of baked potato toppings, and wonderful fillings for "twice-baked" potatoes.

Boiled Potatoes

As mentioned in "Kitchen Tips" (p. 54) save water in which potatoes have been boiled to use in soups, stews, and gravies, and in baking. It is full of nourishment.

BONELESS BOILED POTATOES I

The "bone" of a potato is the partially-cooked hard center that sometimes results from standard boiling methods. What follows is the traditional method, dating from the 18th century, that eliminates this core.

Let potatoes boil in water for 5 minutes, then pour off water. Refill the pot with *cold* water, and return pot to heat, bringing it again to a boil. Simmer for 20 to 25 minutes, drain, and serve. (By replacing the boiling water with cold part way through the cooking process, the inside of the potato continues to cook while the outside layers are cooled off and slowed down. By the time the outside is nicely done, therefore, the inside is also ready.)

BONELESS BOILED POTATOES II

For those who like their potatoes less moist — "mealy."

Put potatoes in cold water and bring to a boil. Boil gently until potatoes are cooked through. Pour off water, leaving the potatoes in the pot. Cover pot with clean folded dish towel. Turn off the burner and replace pot on the still hot burner. Let steam a minute or two, then shake the pot, replace on burner, and reverse the towel, so that the undampened side is over the potatoes. The towel will take up moisture from the cooked potatoes, leaving them pleasantly mealy. Do not let them steam too long, as they will fall apart. Instead, once the proper mealiness is arrived at, keep potatoes hot until serving time over boiling water (in a double boiler), adding butter, parsley, or chives as desired.

BOILED POTATOES

A method utilizing the moisture contained in the potatoes themselves — and very little water.

In heavy kettle or saucepan with lid, place desired number of potatoes in about 1 inch of water. Cover tightly and bring contents to boil. Boil over medium heat until potatoes are tender. If lid does not fit tightly, check during cooking to see that potatoes have not boiled dry. Boil whole potatoes 30 to 40 minutes, cut potatoes 15 to 20 minutes.

IRISH BONY METHOD

This is how the Irish used to make sure their boiled potatoes were hot and tender all the way through, but with slightly crunchy centers. They liked this "bone" at the heart of their staple, and judged cooks by its presence.

Boil potatoes in water to cover for 10 minutes. Drain off water, cover pot with a cloth (a linen tea towel is ideal), and set covered pot in a low oven for about 10 minutes. Serve with cream, melted butter, herbs, or whatever garnish seems best.

Steamed Potatoes

STOVE-TOP STEAMED POTATOES

Steaming potatoes has the virtue of sealing important vitamins and nutrients in the potatoes. But if you need potato cooking water for anything, boiling is the answer.

In bottom of a large kettle or saucepan, place a wire rack or colander. Add just enough water to pot to reach bottom of rack. Bring water to boil, place potatoes (as many as desired) on rack, cover pot, and cook until potatoes are tender. Whole potatoes take 30 to 40 minutes, depending on size; cut potatoes take 20 to 30 minutes. Check water level once or twice during cooking to see that water has not boiled away.

OVEN-STEAMED POTATOES

These potatoes are similar to baked potatoes, but this method produces a moist skin, rather than the crusty, chewy skin of true baked potatoes.

Wash potatoes and pierce each deeply with a fork. Wrap each potato in aluminum foil and place packages on oven racks or cookie sheets. Gauge cooking time and temperature according to size of potatoes and what else is in the oven. Medium potatoes will take about 60 minutes at 400°F., 70 minutes at 350°F., and 90 minutes at 325°F.

KITCHEN TIPS FOR POTATOES

To keep boiled potatoes fresh and white, add 1 teaspoon cream of tartar to cooking water.

If time is short, boil potatoes for 5 minutes before baking them. Then pierce and bake for half the usual time; they will be perfect.

For fluffy mashed potatoes, keep heat on low under pan while mashing, and continue cooking and stirring until all excess water has evaporated. Then lightly blend in milk.

Hot milk, instead of cold, makes mashed potatoes even smoother.

Cook and eat potatoes in their skins, or save the peels and fry or toast them; save all the vitamins you can.

A pinch of sugar, instead of salt, in water for boiling potatoes seals in the vitamin C.

Soaking peeled potatoes ''to preserve color and crispness'' saps them of vitamins, and is unnecessary.

Save water in which potatoes have been cooked, and use it in soups, stews, and gravies — the water is loaded with nutrients.

Sprinkle crushed potato chips on sticky frosting or drippy sauce to absorb excess moisture and hold things together.

Place a piece of raw potato in hot fat for fondu or deep frying to subdue spattering.

Use plain yogurt with chives or mint instead of sour cream to top baked potatoes — far fewer calories and equally delicious taste.

Include a potato in mashed turnips or squash, and the result will be firm instead of watery.

To thicken soups, add 3 tablespoons grated potato for each cup of soup and cook soup until potato disappears, about 15 minutes.

One teaspoon potato flour thickens as well as 1 tablespoon regular flour.

A chunk of potato dropped in too-salty soup or stew will draw out the excess salt and render the dish entirely palatable. Dip out and discard the absorbent potato.

Prick half a potato with holes and use to hold flowers upright in a vase.

A slice of raw potato cleans furniture, silver, paintings, and suede shoes or clothing. Just slice and rub.

Rubbed inside the glass of a scuba mask, a slice of raw potato prevents fogging.

Potato water combed through hair will darken its color. Sunlight makes the process work faster. Use water left from boiling potatoes for this.

Rub skin stained with vegetables such as beets or berries with raw potato to remove stain.

A compress of grated raw potato in a square of gauze, placed on closed eyes for 15 minutes, reduces wrinkles.

Baked Potatoes

Magnificent served right out of the oven with just butter, the baked potato is an example in itself of the marvelous versatility of the "spud." It can be served with a variety of toppings, or it can be "twice-baked," i.e. the pulp can be mashed, various things added to it, then stuffed back into the potato-skin shell, and reheated — a boon to anyone planning a dinner party!

BASIC BAKED POTATOES

Potatoes prepared in this way can be served with any of the delicious toppings that follow or used in the equally attractive "twice-baked" recipes. Gauge your oven temperature and baking time to your needs (see below). For a more tender skin, especially if potatoes are to be "twice-baked," rub the potatoes with butter or cooking oil before baking.

Wash baking potatoes thoroughly and pierce each deeply with a fork. Bake on racks of oven or on cookie sheet until tender. Medium potatoes bake in about 45 minutes at 400°F., 60 minutes at 350°F., 90 minutes at 325°F. Larger potatoes will take longer. Bake them along with whatever else you are baking and gauge the cooking time according to oven temperature. Test potatoes for doneness by squeezing gently: if done, potatoes will be slightly soft. The skin will be nicely crusty.

TWICE-BAKED POTATOES

All of the recipes that follow require the cook to bake the potatoes first (see above), then halve them and scoop out the pulp from each half. The pulp is then mixed with other ingredients, depending on the rule you are following, packed back into the waiting potato-skin halves, and reheated at 350°F. for 20 to 30 minutes, or until heated through. Each recipe is sufficient for 4 baked potatoes (8 halves). Twice-baking times given are geared to cold potatoes. If you put hot potatoes and hot stuffing back into the oven to reheat, you need only 10 to 15 minutes at the temperature given. Please note that some fillings — Seafood-Cheese, Au Gratin, Meat, and Oyster — can provide sufficient protein for a meal, in addition to being a unique addition to a fancy formal dinner menu. Thus, they can be usefully served as a main course, supplemented only by a vegetable or salad when you are pressed for time.

Sour Cream and Onion Filling:
½ cup sour cream

2 tablespoons butter

2 teaspoons minced onion

3 slices bacon, cooked and crumbled

Bake at 350°F. for 20 to 30 minutes.

Seafood-Cheese Filling:
1 pound cooked fish or shrimp, chopped

2 tablespoons butter

1 cup hot milk

Pepper

½ teaspoon salt

2 tablespoons minced onion

⅔ cup grated Swiss or cheddar cheese

Bake 25 to 30 minutes at 375°F.

Au Gratin Filling:
1 cup grated American, Swiss, or cheddar cheese

Bake at 350°F. for 20 to 25 minutes.

Nippy Filling:
2 teaspoons prepared mustard

1 small minced onion

1 tablespoon Worcestershire sauce

Salt to taste (½ teaspoon)

1 cup bread crumbs

2 tablespoons melted butter

Combine first 4 ingredients with potato pulp, replace, and sprinkle tops with mixture of bread crumbs and butter. Bake at 350°F. for 25 to 30 minutes or until crumb topping is crusty and brown.

Meat Filling:
2 cups finely chopped cooked meat

1 clove garlic, crushed

1 small onion, chopped

Salt and pepper to taste

2 teaspoons chopped fresh parsley

Bake at 350°F. for 25 to 30 minutes, or until filling is piping hot and lightly browned.

Oyster Filling:

8 large uncooked oysters
¼ cup French dressing
½ cup buttered bread crumbs
4 tablespoons butter

½ teaspoon salt
Pepper
¼ teaspoon paprika
¼ cup cream

Marinate oysters in French dressing for ½ hour. Meanwhile, beat pulp with butter, salt, pepper, paprika, and cream. Pile pulp back in shells and make a hollow in each half. Put 1 oyster in each hollow. Sprinkle with buttered crumbs and bake 20 to 25 minutes at 350°F.

Lima-Cheese Filling:

1 cup cooked lima beans
½ cup grated sharp cheese

Bake 20 to 25 minutes at 350°F.

Amandine Filling:

½ cup grated sharp cheese
2 tablespoons butter
¼ cup minced celery
¼ cup chopped blanched almonds
1 cup milk

1 tablespoon flour
1 tablespoon minced onion
Salt and pepper to taste
Paprika

Bake 30 to 40 minutes at 350°F.

Cottage Filling:

1 cup cottage cheese
½ cup milk or buttermilk
1 tablespoon minced onion

Salt and pepper to taste
2 teaspoons chopped chives
Paprika

Beat together all ingredients except paprika with potato pulp until mixture is light and fluffy. Divide mixture evenly among 8 shells. Sprinkle with paprika. Bake at 350°F. until lightly browned and heated through.

Russian Filling:

2 tablespoons Russian dressing
1½ teaspoons Worcestershire sauce
2 tablespoons minced onion, sautéed

1 teaspoon baking powder
⅓ cup buttermilk

Bake at 350°F. until lightly browned and heated through.

Sausage Filling:

Substitute cooked sausages for oysters in Oyster Filling recipe.

Peanut-Butter Filling:

½ cup peanut butter   ¼ cup hot milk
½ teaspoon salt   2 stiffly-beaten egg whites
Pepper to taste

Combine potato pulp with first 4 ingredients, then gently fold in egg whites. Replace in skins and bake 20 to 25 minutes at 350° F.

Pinnacle Filling:

¼ cup plus 2 tablespoons light cream   Salt to taste
¾ tablespoon grated onion   Caviar

Mash potato pulp until smooth, then stir in cream, onion, and salt. Beat until fluffy. Pile pulp back in shells and bake at 350°F. until heated through. Serve topped with caviar.

TOPPINGS FOR BAKED POTATOES

Bacon bits
Caviar
Chopped onion and freshly
  ground black pepper
Chopped pimiento-green
  pepper mixture
Grated cheese — cheddar,
  Parmesan, Gruyère,
  American
Herbed butter
Herbed gravy
Lemon butter
Marinated chopped
  mushrooms

Mixed dried herbs —
  parsley, chives, basil,
  dill, oregano, thyme
Peanut butter and
  crumbled bacon
Plain yogurt, or herbed
  yogurt
Poppy seeds
Sour cream and chives
Toasted sesame seeds
Tomato sauce

Fried Potatoes

Potatoes can be deep fried, oven fried, or pan fried — and will taste different according to the method used. For best results, we recommend you peel potatoes to be fried.

DEEP FRYING

To obtain tender crunchy crispness without greasiness, the secret is to cook the potato pieces as quickly as possible in fat that is just the right temperature.

Use a pot or deep saucepan with a flat bottom. A 3-quart pan requires about 3 pounds of fat (3 pints cooking oil) — enough to cover the potatoes without crowding them with plenty of room for bubbling. Do not fill the pot more than half full of fat, and use a metal frying basket for quick and easy removal of the cooked potatoes.

Bring the fat up to a temperature of 375°F. gradually. Gradual heating lets any moisture escape slowly without exploding. Should a fire erupt, smother it with a metal lid or with salt or baking soda. NEVER throw water on a fat fire.

Test the fat temperature with a thermometer for best results. If none is available, drop in a cube of bread. If it takes 60 seconds to become crisp and brown, fat is about 375°F. When the fat has reached 375°F., fry the potatoes in small batches, allowing the fat to reheat briefly in between. Skim out bits of potato between batches. Frying in small batches gives each piece room to cook, and does not cool off the fat too rapidly.

Slice mature baking potatoes into desired shapes and soak them in very cold water for half an hour before cooking. This cold water bath makes them crisp and helps ensure they will cook up crisp. Drain and dry the pieces thoroughly before immersing in hot fat.

Lower potatoes into hot fat slowly. Cook until crisply browned — 5 minutes or less — remove, and drain on absorbent paper. Salt to taste, and keep warm in paper-lined plate in oven.

OVEN FRYING

A more care-free method.

Preheat oven to 450°F. Slice medium baking potatoes into slices or pieces ¼ inch thick. Soak in cold water for half an hour, then drain and pat dry with paper towel. Melt 1 tablespoon of butter, or use 1 tablespoon of cooking oil, per potato; stir into dried potato pieces to coat thoroughly. Spread pieces in single layer on baking sheet. Bake about 20 minutes, turning pieces over several times to brown all sides. Potatoes are done when they have turned a rich crispy brown. Sprinkle with salt and serve. Allow 1 medium potato per person.

PAN FRYING

Great for breakfasts or brunches.

Cut up medium baking potatoes into desired shapes. Melt one tablespoon butter, or use 1 tablespoon cooking oil, per potato in large frying pan. Add potatoes and fry, stirring frequently and turning pieces over, until all pieces are nicely brown, crusty, and cooked through. Salt and serve. Allow 1 medium potato per person.

EXTRA-CRISP FRIED POTATOES

Chilling the potatoes between first and second fryings is the secret to the crispest fries imaginable.

1 large potato per person
2 cups cooking oil for frying
Salt

Peel potatoes and cut into desired shapes — strips, rounds, or slices. Dry pieces on paper towel. Heat oil in large frying pan to 350°F. Fry potatoes for 5 minutes, remove with slotted spoon, and drain on paper towel. Place potatoes in refrigerator for half an hour to chill. Reheat oil to 375°F. and place chilled potatoes back in it to fry for 5 more minutes. Turn potatoes so they brown evenly, remove, and drain. Sprinkle with salt and serve with catsup, mayonnaise, and/or mustard.

PUFFY FRIED POTATOES

These are like chips, only better.

6 medium potatoes
Fat for deep frying
Salt

Peel potatoes and slice ⅛ inch thick. Drain and dry carefully. Fry in deep fat heated to 275°F. about 10 minutes, or until lightly browned. Drain and cool slices. Heat fat to 390°F. and put slices back in. They should puff up right away. Remove from fat, drain, sprinkle with salt, and serve. Serves 6.

SARATOGA CHIPS

The original potato-chip recipe, or so they say.

6 medium potatoes
Fat for deep frying
Salt

Peel potatoes and slice very thin. Drain and dry. Plunge slices into rapidly boiling water, drain, and dry. Immerse in deep fat (375°F.) and fry until golden and crisp, 3 to 5 minutes. Drain, sprinkle with salt, and serve. Serves 6.

POTATO FRITTERS

A delicious elaboration on the basic chip idea.

4 medium potatoes
1¼ cups sifted flour
¼ teaspoon salt
1 egg

1 cup milk
Fat for deep frying
Salt

Peel potatoes. Cut potatoes into slices ⅛ inch thick. Mix together flour and ¼ teaspoon salt, then beat in egg and milk to form a smooth batter. Dip potato slices in batter, then fry in hot fat (385°F.) until crisp and brown. Drain on absorbent paper, sprinkle with salt, and serve. Serves 4.

POTATO PUFFS

Celestial and puffy as a cloud.

½ cup flour
1 teaspoon baking powder
¼ teaspoon salt
1 cup mashed potatoes

1 egg, beaten
1 teaspoon minced onion
Fat for deep frying

Combine dry ingredients and stir into potatoes. Stir in egg and onion until mixture is fairly smooth. Drop by large spoonfuls into hot fat (350°F.) and cook 3 to 5 minutes, until balls puff and turn brown. Drain and serve. Serves 4.

POTATO CHEESE FRITTERS

Wonderful way to use leftover mashed potatoes.

2 cups mashed potatoes
½ cup grated sharp cheese
1 egg
Salt and pepper to taste
1 tablespoon minced onion

2 tablespoons melted butter
1 egg, beaten
1 cup bread crumbs
Fat for frying

Combine first 6 ingredients and stir to blend thoroughly. Shape into rectangles, dip in beaten egg, then in bread crumbs, and fry in deep fat (or in skillet) until crusty and brown. Serves 4.

PAN FRIES

Good and chunky. Great with eggs for breakfast.

1 garlic clove
3 tablespoons butter or bacon fat
8 medium potatoes, cut into bite-size
   chunks

¼ cup minced onion
Salt and pepper to taste

Rub frying pan with garlic clove and discard clove. Melt butter and sauté potatoes and onion slowly, turning mixture frequently, until potatoes are brown all over and tender all the way through — about 20 minutes. Season with salt and pepper. Serves 8.

HASH BROWNS

Use raw or leftover baked or boiled potatoes for this.

1 small onion, chopped
3 tablespoons butter or bacon fat
2 medium potatoes, diced or cubed

1 tablespoon flour
Salt and pepper to taste

Sauté onion in melted butter or bacon fat until brown. Sprinkle potatoes with flour and add to frying pan. Brown them quickly, turning several times with fork or spatula. Season with salt and pepper. When nicely brown, pile into a mound in pan and let crust form on bottom. Turn mound over and let crust form under other side. Lift out onto plate and serve. Serves 4.

CHICKEN-FRIED POTATOES

These fries are extra-specially crunchy. They come from down South, but taste good anywhere.

4 medium potatoes
1 egg

1 cup bread crumbs, seasoned with
   salt and pepper
Fat for deep frying

Peel potatoes and cut into strips ¼ inch thick. Beat egg slightly and dip potatoes first in egg, then in seasoned bread crumbs. Fry in deep fat until crisp and brown, 3 to 5 minutes. Drain and serve. Serves 4-6.

SNACKS AND HORS D'OEUVRES

Some interesting tidbits to make from potatoes.

TOASTY PEELS

What a snack! Tasty, toasty, and nutritious, too! Save all your peelings and keep a constant supply of these on hand.

Peelings from well-scrubbed
   potatoes
Melted butter, ½ cup for each
   2 to 3 cups of peels

Salt

Preheat oven to 350°F. Spread peels on greased flat pan so that they do not touch each other. Drizzle melted butter over peels, then sprinkle with salt to taste. Bake about 15 minutes, until peels are crunchy-crisp. Serve hot with tomato juice or cocktails.

Variation:

Sprinkle ½ cup grated cheese over baked peels, return pan to oven just until cheese melts, and serve hot.

FRIED PEELS

Also a great snack.

Peelings from well-scrubbed
   potatoes

Fat for deep frying
Salt

Dip peels into hot fat until they become crisp and brown — about 3 to 5 minutes. Drain, sprinkle with salt, and serve.

STUFFED MUSHROOMS

Guests will gobble these up in a trice.

1 pound mushrooms (about 30
   good-sized ones)
¾ cup mashed potatoes

¼ cup cottage cheese
2 tablespoons minced onion
1 teaspoon Worcestershire sauce

Preheat oven to 375°F. Wash mushrooms and remove stems. Set caps aside. Chop stems and combine with remaining ingredients. Spoon into mushroom caps. Place caps in greased flat pan and bake 10 to 15 minutes, until bubbly and cooked through. Serve immediately. Makes 30 stuffed caps.

EASY CHEESIES

Hot from the oven, these will be the hit of the party.

½ cup mashed potatoes
3 tablespoons sharp cheese spread
2 tablespoons butter
2 tablespoons flour

½ teaspoon salt
1 tablespoon cold water
Paprika

Combine all ingredients except paprika and blend thoroughly. Knead with fork or fingers 2 minutes. Shape into long roll about 1 inch in diameter, wrap, and chill for 2 hours.

Preheat oven to 425°F. Remove wrap and slice roll into ⅛-inch slices. Lay slices on ungreased cookie sheet, dust with paprika, and bake for 10 minutes, or until golden. Makes about 36 cheesies.

SKORDALIA

A most unforgettable dip from Greece. It packs a garlicky wallop, so make sure everyone eats some. Pita bread, vegetables, or plain crackers are all good to dunk in this. It can also be used as a sauce for fish.

2 cups mashed potatoes
½ teaspoon garlic powder, or
   3 cloves fresh garlic, crushed

½ cup mayonnaise
1 teaspoon vinegar
½ teaspoon salt

Mix all ingredients well by hand or in blender. Chill and use for dip, or heat carefully over boiling water and use for sauce over fish. Makes about 2½ cups.

PIROSHKI

Boiled or baked Russian-style turnovers that can be filled with any number of things.

Dough:
3 cups flour
¾ cup mashed potatoes
1 egg
½ teaspoon salt

½ to ¾ cup milk, or enough
   to form stiff dough
1 egg, beaten

Preheat oven to 350°F. Blend flour and potatoes to form coarse meal. Work in salt and egg thoroughly, then add just enough milk to form a dough that is firm but rolls easily. Place on lightly-floured board and roll to ¼-inch thickness. Cut dough into 3-inch squares, or use a large biscuit cutter to cut it into 3- to 4-inch circles. Mound filling on half of dough, fold over other half, and seal. Make decorative incision in top of piroshki, paint with beaten egg. Bake on greased sheet 8 to 15 minutes, depending on filling, or until filling is done and dough is crisp and brown. Or drop filled piroshki into rapidly boiling water, cover, and cook 8 to 12 minutes. Serve topped with lots of butter. Makes about 3 dozen piroshki.

Fillings:
3 cups blueberries
¼ cup sugar

or:
1 head cabbage, chopped and sautéed lightly in butter
1 tablespoon caraway seeds

or:
1 can (16 ounces) salmon, drained and flaked
3 hard-boiled eggs, cut up
½ cup heavy cream
1 tablespoon dill
½ teaspoon pepper

or:
2 cups cottage cheese
1 egg
½ cup mashed potatoes
Salt and pepper

or:
1 pound ground beef, browned
1 medium onion, minced and sautéed
Salt and pepper
½ cup green pepper, chopped and sautéed

WRAPPED SAUSAGE

Serve these whole for a tasty supper. Or slice into 2-inch lengths before baking and serve as hors d'oeuvres.

1 cup flour
¼ teaspoon salt
4 tablespoons butter
⅓ cup mashed potatoes

2 to 3 tablespoons ice water
½ pound sausage links (about 6)
1 egg white

Preheat oven to 350°F. Combine flour and salt and cut in butter. Cut in potatoes to form a coarse meal. Stir in just enough ice water, a tablespoon at a time, to hold dough together. Roll dough out on pastry board to ⅛-inch thickness. Cut into 3-inch squares. Lay a sausage link on each piece of dough and roll dough around sausage. Seal ends with egg white. Place rolls, seam side down, on greased baking sheet and brush with egg white. Make several cuts in pastry to let steam escape. Bake until pastry is brown and sausage is done, 35 to 40 minutes. Makes 6 rolls.

POTATOES IN SOUP

An international fixation — we have oyster stew and clam chowder; the French invented Vichyssoise. A host of countries pride themselves on their own versions of potato soup. Ecuador, Holland, Hungary, and Poland are here represented, as is good old-fashioned down-home America.

VICHYSSOISE

The legendary potato soup of France in a version more seasoned than some. Even better if made and refrigerated a day or two before serving.

¼ cup butter, preferably unsalted
4 leeks, white part only, minced
1 small onion, chopped
2 sprigs fresh parsley
½ cup chopped celery
2 medium potatoes, peeled and
   sliced thin

Salt and pepper to taste
4 cups chicken stock or chicken
   broth
Dash nutmeg or curry powder
Dash Worcestershire sauce
1 cup heavy cream
Chopped chives or dill

Melt butter in heavy saucepan. Add leeks and onion and cook very slowly until tender but not brown. Add all other ingredients *except* cream and cook 20 to 25 minutes, until potatoes are tender. Put through fine sieve or puree in blender. Stir in cream, reheat, and serve hot, or chill thoroughly and serve cold. Garnish with chopped chives or fresh dill. Serves 4.

CREAMY POTATO SOUP

The essential potato soup. Vary its flavor by adding different seasonings or pureed vegetables.

6 medium potatoes
1 small onion, grated
1½ quarts water
1 teaspoon salt

1½ cups light cream
Dash pepper
Chopped chives, crumbled bacon, or
   grated cheese

Peel and dice potatoes. Put in large saucepan with onion, water, and salt. Boil 15 to 20 minutes, until tender. Pour off and save water. Mash potatoes. Combine potato cooking water and cream and heat to boiling. Stir in potatoes and pepper. Garnish with chives, bacon, or cheese. Serves 6-8.

CHUNKY POTATO SOUP

This soup is good with a cup or so of leftover vegetables added.

2 tablespoons butter
1 tablespoon chopped onion
1 tablespoon minced fresh parsley
1 tablespoon chopped celery
3 medium potatoes, diced

1 quart boiling water
1 tablespoon flour
½ teaspoon salt
¼ teaspoon white pepper
Chives or seasoned croutons

In heavy soup pot, melt 1 tablespoon butter and sauté onion, parsley, and celery until lightly browned. Add potatoes, cover pot, and cook for 2 minutes. Pour in water, cover, and simmer 1 hour. In small saucepan, melt remaining tablespoon of butter and stir in flour. Dip out a cup of potato cooking water and slowly stir into flour mixture. Add seasonings and stir until mixture thickens. Pour into potato pot and stir to blend. Add salt and pepper. Serve topped with chives or croutons. Serves 4-6.

POTATO CHOWDER

Add a cup or two of cooked fish, if you wish, to this hearty soup.

½ cup diced salt pork
2 cups diced potatoes
1 cup diced turnip
1 cup diced carrot
½ cup minced onion
½ cup chopped celery

½ cup diced green pepper
2 to 3 cups boiling water
1 tablespoon butter
1 tablespoon flour
2 cups chicken broth
Salt and pepper to taste

Fry salt pork until crisp and brown. Remove pork bits and sauté vegetables in fat until lightly colored. Pour in boiling water to cover and cook until vegetables are tender, about 20 to 25 minutes. In small saucepan, melt butter and stir in flour. Slowly pour in broth, stirring constantly, and continue to cook, stirring, until mixture thickens slightly. Pour into vegetable mixture, stir to blend, and add seasonings. Serves 6-8.

DUTCH DUMPLING POTATO SOUP

Eggy dumplings top this tempting soup.

8 medium potatoes, cubed
1 quart milk
½ teaspoon salt
¼ teaspoon pepper

1 tablespoon butter
½ cup flour
1 egg, well beaten
¼ cup milk

Boil potatoes until tender, about 20 to 25 minutes. Drain. Add milk and heat thoroughly, but do not boil. Stir in seasonings. In separate bowl, blend butter and flour with fingertips or pastry blender then stir in egg and milk. Drop dumplings by teaspoonfuls onto hot soup, cover, and cook 10 minutes. Serves 4.

POTATO-SALMON CHOWDER

Pink and pretty, this is a whole meal in itself.

5 medium potatoes, cut up
2 medium carrots, sliced
3 cups water
1 teaspoon salt
1 10-ounce package frozen peas
1 small onion, chopped
1 cup chopped celery

3 tablespoons butter
¼ cup flour
5 cups milk
1 1-pound can salmon, skin and
  bones removed
Dash Worcestershire sauce

Combine potatoes, carrots, water, and salt in saucepan and simmer about 15 minutes, until potatoes are tender. Add peas, bring to boil, cover pan, and remove from heat. Drain.

In skillet, sauté onion and celery in butter until tender. Stir in flour and cook, stirring, for 1 minute. Gradually stir in 2½ cups milk and stir over low heat until mixture thickens.

Mix salmon and liquid from can with cooked vegetables, then pour in flour mixture, Worcestershire sauce, and remaining 2½ cups milk. Heat almost to boiling and serve. Serves 8-10.

OYSTER STEW

Traditional New England fare that is divine with raised biscuits.

2 medium potatoes, diced
1 teaspoon salt
1 cup water
1 pint oysters, drained and cut up
1 pint oyster liquid (add milk if
  necessary to make up volume)

3 tablespoons butter
1 cup light cream
Dash white pepper
Paprika

Boil potatoes, salt, and water for 10 minutes. Add oysters and oyster liquid and heat briefly. Remove from heat as mixture is about to boil and stir in butter, cream, and pepper. Return to low heat until hot. Do not boil. Let stand, covered, 15 minutes, then dust with paprika and serve. Serves 6.

POLISH POTATO SOUP

Try this with thick slabs of well-buttered dark rye bread.

4 medium potatoes, cubed	½ teaspoon caraway seeds
6 cups water	1 tablespoon flour
½ teaspoon salt	1 cup sour cream

Combine potatoes, water, salt, and caraway seeds in large saucepan and boil for 15 to 20 minutes, until potatoes are tender. Combine ½ cup of potato liquid with flour, stirring to blend thoroughly. Stir flour mixture slowly back into soup. Stir over low heat for 5 minutes. Remove from heat and stir in sour cream. Serve immediately. Serves 6-8.

POTATO-TOMATO SOUP

Pink, creamy, and luscious.

2 medium onions, sliced	2 teaspoons sugar
4 tablespoons butter	½ teaspoon salt
2 medium potatoes, peeled and sliced	Dash paprika
6 cups boiling water	¼ teaspoon dried basil
5 medium fresh tomatoes, sliced, or 3 cups canned tomatoes	1 cup light cream

Sauté onions in butter until tender. Add to potatoes and boiling water in soup kettle and simmer, covered, about 20 to 25 minutes. Add tomatoes, sugar, salt, paprika, and basil and simmer, covered, another 20 minutes. Force through fine sieve or puree soup in blender. Bring soup to boiling. Remove from heat and stir in cream. Serves 6-8.

AJIACO

Ecuador's potato soup.

4 small onions, chopped	½ teaspoon salt
¼ cup butter	Dash pepper
2 tablespoons flour	3 cups milk, scalded
1½ cups beef consommé	½ cup cooked green peas
1½ cups water	3 eggs
4 medium potatoes, diced	4 ounces cream cheese, softened
Dash saffron or turmeric	1 ripe avocado, peeled and sliced

Sauté onions in butter until tender. Stir in flour and blend until smooth. Gradually pour in consommé and water, stirring constantly. Bring mixture to boil and add potatoes and seasonings. Simmer 20 minutes. Stir in milk and peas and simmer 5 minutes longer. Beat eggs into cream cheese and beat ½ cup hot soup into mixture. Slowly pour cheese mixture into hot soup, stirring constantly. Divide avocado slices evenly among 8 soup bowls and fill bowls with hot soup. Serves 8.

DILL SOUP

Dill soup tastes as fresh as springtime. Save the potatoes and use them in another dish.

3 medium potatoes, quartered	1 cup sour cream
3 cups boiling lightly salted water	½ cup chopped fresh dill (1 large
2 tablespoons flour	bunch)
¼ cup cold water	1 egg yolk, beaten

Cook potatoes in boiling water for 20 minutes. Lift out potatoes and save for some other purpose.

Place 2 cups potato water in saucepan. Stir flour into cold water, then blend with sour cream. Stir this into potato water. Stir in dill and cook, stirring constantly, until soup boils and thickens slightly. Stir small amount of soup into beaten egg yolk, then pour yolk slowly into soup, stirring continually. Blend thoroughly. Chill soup and serve garnished with sprigs of dill. If soup is too thick, thin with milk before serving. Serves 4-6.

FISH CHOWDER

The essence of Down East cooking.

4 medium potatoes, diced	1 quart milk
¼ pound salt pork, diced	Salt and pepper to taste
2 small onions, minced	2 tablespoons butter
2 pounds fresh cod, boned and cut in	
pieces	

Boil potatoes in enough water to cover for 10 minutes. Fry salt pork until fat is rendered and bits are crisp. Remove and reserve pork bits. Fry onion in fat to golden color. Place fish, pork bits, onions, potatoes and water, and milk in soup kettle. Bring slowly to simmer and let simmer 1 hour. Season to taste, add butter and let it melt, and serve piping hot with plain crackers. Serves 10-12.

CAPE ANNE CLAM CHOWDER

This is the rich version bursting with clams every New Englander knows and loves.

1-inch cube salt pork, diced	Liquor from clams, plus water to
1 medium onion, minced	make 2 cups
2 medium potatoes, diced	2 cups milk
2 cups water	Salt and pepper to taste
1 pint shucked clams, cleaned and	1 tablespoon butter
cut up	

Fry salt pork until fat is rendered and bits are crisp. Remove and reserve pork bits. Add onion and sauté to a golden color. In large saucepan, boil potatoes in water and clam liquor 15 to 20 minutes, until potatoes are tender. Add pork bits, onion, clams, milk, and seasonings and heat *almost* to boiling. Float butter on chowder and let it melt. Serve with fresh biscuits or corn bread. Serves 4-6.

MANHATTAN CLAM CHOWDER

The red version indigenous to points south of New England.

1 pint shucked clams, cleaned and
   cut up
Liquor from clams, plus water to
   make 2 cups
2 medium potatoes, diced
3 medium carrots, diced

4 stalks celery, chopped
1 16-ounce can tomatoes
2 strips bacon, chopped into ½-inch
   strips and fried until crisp
½ teaspoon dried thyme
Salt and pepper to taste

In large kettle, combine all ingredients. Bring slowly to boil and simmer,
covered, for 30 minutes. Serves 4-6.

MEATBALL SOUP

*Top this with little dumplings (p. 123 ff.), or serve with crusty French bread, and
it's a whole meal.*

2 medium potatoes, cubed
2 medium carrots, sliced
1 medium onion, chopped
2 cups chopped celery, with tops
1 16-ounce can tomatoes, or 4
   medium fresh tomatoes, peeled
   and chopped

3 cups water
¾ pound lean ground beef
1 egg
½ cup bread crumbs
¼ cup chopped fresh parsley
Salt and pepper to taste

In soup kettle, combine potatoes, carrots, onion, celery, tomatoes, and
water. Simmer, covered, for 30 minutes. In separate bowl, combine ground
beef, egg, bread crumbs, parsley, and seasonings. Shape into 1-inch balls and
drop into soup. Cover soup and simmer for 15 minutes, or until meatballs are
tender. Add dumplings, if desired, at same time meatballs are dropped in.
Serves 4-6.

MUSHROOM POTATO SOUP

An intriguing soup rife with the flavor of fresh mushrooms.

½ pound fresh mushrooms, chopped
1 small onion, minced
1 tablespoon butter
3 tablespoons flour
5 cups water

2 medium potatoes, cubed
2 teaspoons Worcestershire sauce
1 tablespoon lemon juice
Salt and pepper to taste
Chopped fresh chives or dill

In large kettle, sauté mushrooms and onion in butter until onion becomes
translucent and mushrooms have given up liquid. Sprinkle flour over
mixture and stir in. Cook 2 minutes more. Stir in water, 1 cup at a time, and
cook, stirring, until mixture boils and thickens. Stir in potatoes,
Worcestershire sauce, lemon juice, salt, and pepper. Cover and simmer for
45 to 50 minutes, until potatoes are good and tender. Serve garnished with
chopped chives or dill. Serves 8-10.

HUNGARIAN POTATO SOUP

Pimiento and paprika add a colorful fillip.

4 tablespoons butter
3 medium potatoes, diced
2 stalks celery, diced
1 medium onion, minced
1 pimiento, minced

2 tablespoons chopped fresh parsley
4 cups chicken broth
1½ cups sour cream
½ teaspoon paprika

Melt butter in soup kettle or large saucepan and sauté potatoes, celery, onion, and pimiento until lightly colored. Stir in parsley and broth and simmer, covered, 20 to 25 minutes, until potatoes are tender. Remove pan from heat and stir in sour cream and paprika. Serve at once. Serves 4-6.

CHEESE AND POTATO SOUP

Cheese perks up the flavor of this basic potato soup and turns it into a unique creation. Taste will vary with the type of cheese used.

3 medium potatoes
2 cups boiling salted water
2 to 3 cups milk
1 medium onion, minced
3 tablespoons butter
2 tablespoons flour

½ teaspoon salt
¼ teaspoon paprika
2 cups grated cheese (cheddar,
    American, Swiss, or whatever)
Chopped parsley

Cook potatoes in boiling water until tender — 20 to 25 minutes. Drain, reserving potato water; peel and mash potatoes. Add milk to reserved water to total 1 quart.

Sauté onion in butter in soup kettle until lightly colored, then stir in flour. Slowly stir in milk and water mixture. Add potatoes and seasonings and cook, stirring, until mixture almost boils. Sprinkle cheese on top and slowly stir it in until it melts completely. Do not boil. Serve garnished with parsley. Serves 6-8.

ARTICHOKE SOUP

Different and delicious.

1 tablespoon butter
1 medium potato, sliced thin
½ medium onion, sliced
2 cups chopped watercress
2 cups chopped parsley
1 4-ounce can artichoke hearts in
    water, chopped

1 cup chicken broth
1 tablespoon chopped fresh dill
2 cups milk
Salt and pepper to taste
Watercress, parsley, or dill

Melt butter in soup kettle and sauté potato and onion until tender. Add watercress, parsley, artichoke hearts, chicken broth, and dill and simmer, covered, for 15 minutes. Stir in milk, season with salt and pepper, and simmer 1 minute. Puree soup in blender and serve hot or cold. Garnish with sprigs of watercress, parsley, or dill. Serves 4.

JUST POTATOES

An amazing variety of casseroles can be made by adding just a little something to the basic potato, used mashed, fried, grated, or boiled, cut-up or whole — all tasting and looking like quite different foods.

Mashed Potato Dishes

GARLIC POTATOES

A rich, savory side dish for any kind of roast.

6 medium potatoes
2 tablespoons butter
2 eggs, beaten
2 tablespoons flour

1 clove garlic, minced
2 tablespoons chopped parsley
Nutmeg, salt, pepper to taste

Preheat oven to 350°F. Boil and mash potatoes. Stir in butter. Combine remaining ingredients and stir into potatoes. Place in greased 1½-quart baking dish and bake 25 to 30 minutes, until lightly browned. Drizzle melted butter over top. Serves 6.

TENDEREST MASHED POTATOES

A method often used in Ireland, it produces potatoes of pearly whiteness and airy lightness.

8 medium potatoes
Milk

Salt and pepper
4 tablespoons butter (or bacon fat)

Peel and quarter potatoes. Place in heavy saucepan and pour in enough milk to half cover them. Cook over medium heat until tender (15 to 20 minutes), mash, and season. Pile in serving bowl and make a deep well in center. Pour in melted butter. Dip forkfuls of potato in butter. Serves 6-8.

POTATOES CHANTILLY

A speedy path to luxury.

3 cups hot seasoned mashed potatoes
½ cup heavy cream

½ cup grated Swiss, cheddar, or
Parmesan cheese

Pile hot seasoned mashed potatoes in greased baking dish. Heat oven to 450°F. Whip cream until stiff and pile on top of potatoes. Sprinkle top with grated cheese. Stick in hot oven to melt cheese and brown top lightly (about 10 minutes). Serves 6-8.

POTATOES SMETANA

Potatoes mashed in sour cream.

6 medium potatoes
1 cup sour cream
1 tablespoon grated onion

Salt and pepper to taste
2 tablespoons butter

Steam or boil potatoes, then peel and mash them. Whip mashed pulp with sour cream and onion, then stir in salt and pepper. Pile into 1½-quart baking dish, dot with butter, and bake at 375°F. 10 to 15 minutes, until top is lightly browned. Serves 6.

GARLIC AND CHILI POTATOES

A rich and spicy dish from Peru, original home of the potato.

8 medium potatoes
3 tablespoons butter or cooking oil
6 scallions, with green part, chopped
4 cloves garlic, crushed
1 teaspoon or more chili powder
Salt and pepper to taste

1 cup milk
½ cup water
½ pound Longhorn, Monterey Jack, or other mild cheese, grated
4 hard-boiled eggs, chopped

Steam potatoes, peel, and mash while still hot. In large pot, melt butter or oil and sauté scallions. Stir in crushed garlic, chili, salt, and pepper. When scallions are tender, add mashed potatoes, milk, and water. Cook, stirring, until ingredients are well blended. Stir in grated cheese and chopped eggs and continue to heat until cheese melts. Serve over rice. Serves 8.

ORANGEY POTATOES

Delicious with roast duck or pork.

6 medium potatoes
2 tablespoons butter
⅔ cup milk, heated

Salt to taste
½ cup orange juice
1 tablespoon grated orange rind

Preheat oven to 350°F. Steam or boil potatoes until tender, then peel and mash. Whip pulp with butter, milk, salt, and juice until fluffy. Pile in greased 1½-quart baking dish, sprinkle with orange rind, and bake 10 to 15 minutes, until top is lightly browned. Serves 4-6.

MASHED POTATOES AND CHESTNUTS

A festive holiday dish to serve with Thanksgiving turkey.

1 pound chestnuts
3 medium potatoes
Salt and pepper to taste

2 tablespoons butter
1 cup milk or cream

Shell, blanch, and peel chestnuts. Peel and cut up potatoes. Steam chestnuts and potatoes separately until tender, 15 to 20 minutes. Drain, combine, and mash or put through food mill. Stir in seasonings, butter, and milk or cream and beat until mixture becomes fluffy. Heat over hot water and serve. Serves 6-8.

POTATO KNISHES

Rich dough wrapped around well-seasoned mashed potatoes. Serve hot or cold. Good with pot roast.

Dough:

2 cups flour
¼ teaspoon salt
1 egg

1 egg white
1 tablespoon cooking oil
½ cup, more or less, cold water

Combine flour and salt and make a hole in middle. Put egg and egg white in hole and mix into flour, adding oil and water as you go until all flour is moistened and dough is slightly sticky. Knead dough until stickiness subsides, then shape into a ball, coat lightly with oil, and place in bowl. Cover and let stand half an hour. Roll out dough on floured board or cloth to form large circle, then pull circle gently with fingers until dough is very thin. Brush surface with oil or melted butter.

Filling:

½ cup minced onion
⅓ cup chicken fat or butter

4 cups mashed potatoes
Salt and pepper

Preheat oven to 400°F. Sauté onion in fat until tender. Combine with remaining ingredients and blend thoroughly. Form filling into roll along one edge of dough and roll dough around it jelly-roll fashion. Slice roll into 2-inch pieces using a knife or the edge of your hand. If you use a knife, push top and bottom dough layers together to seal. Bake on greased sheet 20 to 30 minutes, until dough is nicely browned. Makes 6-8 knishes.

Light 'n Airy

POTATO PUFF

A light and delicious soufflé-like dish.

2 tablespoons butter, melted
2 eggs, separated
1 cup milk

Salt and pepper to taste
2 cups hot mashed potatoes

Preheat oven to 350°F. Blend butter, beaten egg yolks, milk, salt, and pepper with mashed potato. Beat until mixture is very light. In separate bowl, beat egg whites until stiff. Fold gently into potato mixture and place puff in greased and floured 1½-quart baking dish. Bake 10 to 15 minutes, until puff is lightly browned. Serves 4.

FLUFFY OMELET

Add sautéed mushrooms, fines herbes, grated cheese, onions, whatever you like to this omelet. It's most adaptable.

3 eggs, separated
1 cup mashed potatoes

Salt and pepper to taste
3 tablespoons milk or cream

Preheat oven to 325°F. Beat egg yolks. Combine with potatoes and beat until smooth. Beat in seasonings and milk or cream. Whip whites until stiff and fold into potato mixture. Pour mixture into greased skillet with oven-proof handle, top with whatever addition you choose, and bake until firm, about 20 minutes. Fold in half and transfer to serving plate. Serves 2-4.

LEMONY POTATO PUFF

A rather more elegant and very tasty puff.

1 cup dry bread crumbs
¼ cup melted butter
3 eggs, separated
⅓ cup mayonnaise
½ teaspoon salt

1 tablespoon grated lemon rind
2 tablespoons lemon juice
½ cup milk
3 cups mashed potatoes
⅓ cup grated Swiss or cheddar cheese

Preheat oven to 350°F. Mix together bread crumbs and butter and press against bottom and sides of 1½-quart baking dish. Beat egg yolks and combine with mayonnaise, salt, lemon rind, lemon juice, and milk. Beat this mixture into mashed potatoes until smooth and fluffy. In separate bowl, beat egg whites until stiff and fold them gently into potatoes. Pour mixture into crumb-lined casserole. Sprinkle cheese over top and bake 30 to 35 minutes, until casserole is puffy and cheese is browned. Serves 6-8.

POTATO CHEESE SOUFFLE

A cross between cheese soufflé and its potato cousin.

4 eggs, separated
3 tablespoons hot milk
2 tablespoons butter
Salt and pepper to taste

2 teaspoons Worcestershire sauce
½ cup grated cheese
2 cups hot mashed potatoes

Preheat oven to 350°F. Beat egg yolks until light and add with milk, butter, seasonings, and cheese to mashed potatoes. Beat egg whites until stiff and fold into potato mixture. Put soufflé in greased and floured 1½-quart baking dish and bake for 15 to 20 minutes, until top is nicely browned and soufflé has puffed. Serves 4.

POTATO SALMON SOUFFLE

A lovely soft pink cloud.

4 eggs, separated
2 cups hot mashed potatoes
1 cup flaked salmon
1 tablespoon minced pimiento

2 teaspoons minced onion
¼ cup milk
Salt and pepper to taste

Preheat oven to 350°F. Beat yolks until light and blend with potatoes. Stir in salmon, pimiento, onion, milk, and seasonings. Beat egg whites until stiff and fold in. Place mixture in greased baking or soufflé dish and bake 20 to 25 minutes, until lightly browned. Serves 4.

Potato Cakes

POTATO/CHEESE CRUST-CAKE

Surmount this crispy base with creamed cooked vegetables or meat, cut in wedges, and serve.

6 medium potatoes, grated
2 medium onions, grated
3 cups Gruyère or Swiss cheese,
    grated

½ teaspoon salt
Pepper to taste
½ teaspoon nutmeg
Paprika

Preheat oven to 375°F. Combine all ingredients except paprika. Spread mixture in greased 9-inch pie pan or springform pan and dust with paprika. Bake 50 to 60 minutes, until cake is brown and crusty. Serves 6.

POTATO CRISP

Top and bottom of this casserole are brown and crisp and delicious.

¼ cup bacon fat or butter
½ cup dry bread crumbs
1 teaspoon salt
Pepper to taste

1 medium onion, minced
1 egg, beaten
4 medium potatoes, grated

Preheat oven to 400°F. Grease 12x8-inch baking pan with half the fat or butter. Combine crumbs, seasonings, onion, egg, and potatoes, and blend thoroughly. Spread evenly in pan and dot top with remaining butter or bacon fat. Bake in upper third of oven 30 to 40 minutes until top is crusty and brown. Serves 4-6.

POTATOES ANNA

Among the prettiest potato dishes ever invented, although rather complicated to prepare.

4 cups round slices potato, ¼ inch thick, made uniform with biscuit cutter
½ cup butter

2 tablespoons cooking oil
Salt
1 medium onion, grated
½ cup Parmesan cheese

Preheat oven to 375°F. Pat potato rounds dry with paper towel. Melt 2 tablespoons butter in skillet, add oil, and fill bottom of pan with overlapping spirals of potato rounds. Sprinkle with salt, onion, and Parmesan cheese. Shake pan once or twice to prevent potatoes from sticking. Dot top with butter. Cover this layer with a second layer of slices, and sprinkle with salt, onion, cheese, and butter as before. Continue layering slices until all are used up. Cover pan tightly and bake for 45 to 60 minutes, until potatoes are almost done. Turn potatoes at this point and bake 5 to 10 minutes longer, until other side is browned and potatoes are tender. Serves 4-6.

OVEN PANCAKE

Just one big happy pancake.

8 medium potatoes
1 small onion, minced
3 eggs, beaten well

1 cup hot milk
4 tablespoons melted butter
1 teaspoon salt

Preheat oven to 350°F. Grate potatoes and drain off excess moisture. Blend with remaining ingredients and pour into greased shallow baking dish. Bake 50 to 60 minutes, or until top is lightly browned. Serves 6-8.

POTATO CHARLOTTE

Serve this big potato cake with pot roast and gravy, or pork roast and applesauce.

3 tablespoons butter
1 small onion, finely chopped
1 cup cold water
2 slices bread

3 cups grated raw potatoes
2 eggs, beaten
1 teaspoon salt
Paprika

Preheat oven to 400°F. Melt butter in skillet and sauté onion until tender. Pour cold water over bread to soak it thoroughly, then squeeze dry. Combine potatoes, bread, eggs, salt, and onion, and stir to blend thoroughly. Pour into greased baking dish. Dust with paprika and bake 20 to 25 minutes until well browned on top. Serves 4-6.

IRISH POTATO CAKE

Grand with pork or sausage and applesauce.

6 medium potatoes
¼ cup butter
3 eggs
½ teaspoon salt
Pepper
¾ cup flour, sifted before measuring

1 teaspoon cinnamon
½ teaspoon each nutmeg, allspice,
  cloves
1 tablespoon caraway seed
¼ cup milk

Preheat oven to 400°F. Quarter potatoes and cook in water until tender, about 15 to 20 minutes. Drain and mash. Stir in butter, then add eggs, salt, pepper, flour, spices and caraway. Combine thoroughly. Stir in milk to make a fluffy mixture. Place in greased baking dish and bake 30 to 35 minutes, until nicely browned. Serves 6-8.

DUCHESS POTATOES

A royal dish.

4 medium potatoes
¼ cup butter
2 egg yolks, beaten

⅛ teaspoon dry mustard
Salt and pepper to taste
1 egg, beaten

Peel, steam, and mash potatoes. Stir in all but last ingredient and let mixture cool 15 to 20 minutes. Heat oven to 375°F. Pat potato mixture out on floured board and form cakes from it. Put cakes in buttered baking pan and brush lightly with beaten egg. Bake 15 to 20 minutes, until light brown. Serves 4.
(*Note:* If 1 egg yolk and ¼ cup milk are added to the above, Duchess Potatoes can be piped through a pastry tube and used to decorate roasts or serving platters.)

POTATOES NEUFCHATEL

Smoothly and creamily delicious.

3 medium potatoes, cooked and
  mashed
½ cup milk or light cream
1 package (3½ or 4 ounces)
  Neufchâtel cheese

1 egg, beaten
2 tablespoons chopped onion
1 tablespoon chopped fresh parsley
Salt and pepper to taste
Paprika

Preheat oven to 400°F. Combine mashed potatoes, milk, and cheese. Blend until smooth. Stir in egg, onion, and parsley. Season with salt and pepper. Put mixture into greased 1-quart casserole and dust with paprika. Bake 25 to 30 minutes, until piping hot and crusty. Serves 6-8.

LITHUANIAN POTATO LOAF

Add sausage or bacon and applesauce to make this a complete meal, or serve with sauerkraut beside roast pork or sauerbraten. Top with catsup for extra flavor.

½ pound salt pork, diced
1 large onion, minced
12 medium potatoes, grated
¼ cup flour
2 eggs, beaten slightly

¼ cup milk
¼ cup chopped fresh parsley
1 tablespoon minced fresh dill
Salt and pepper to taste

Preheat oven to 350°F. Sauté salt pork until fat is rendered and pieces are crisp and brown. Remove and reserve pork bits, and sauté onion in fat to golden color. Drain excess water from potatoes, pressing against fine sieve to extract as much moisture as possible. (Save water to use in gravy or bread.) Stir flour into potatoes and mix well. Stir in pork bits, onion, and pork fat and blend thoroughly. Stir in remaining ingredients and blend well. Press mixture into greased 8x8-inch baking pan and bake 50 to 60 minutes, until loaf is firm and top is lightly browned. Serves 6-8.

Cut-Up Potatoes

POTATOES DELMONICO

An easy dish with a fancy reputation.

2 tablespoons butter
2 tablespoons flour
2 cups milk
½ teaspoon salt

¼ teaspoon pepper
2 cups diced cooked potatoes
2 tablespoons melted butter
1 cup bread crumbs

Preheat oven to 400°F. Melt butter in heavy saucepan and stir in flour. Gradually stir in milk and seasonings and continue to stir over low heat until mixture thickens. Add diced potatoes. Combine butter and bread crumbs in separate bowl and toss crumbs to coat completely with butter. Pour potatoes into greased baking dish, sprinkle top with buttered crumbs, and bake 15 to 20 minutes, or until top is brown and crisp. Serves 4-6.

POTATOES LYONNAISE

Sometimes called "twice-cooked," they complement a roast nicely.

2 medium potatoes
1 tablespoon minced onion
2 tablespoons butter

Salt and pepper to taste
1 tablespoon chopped parsley

Boil potatoes until they are still slightly crisp, about 10 minutes, then drain, peel, and dice. Sauté onion in butter until tender and add potatoes and seasonings. Cook, stirring, until potatoes are nicely browned. Mound potatoes in serving bowl and sprinkle with chopped parsley. Serves 4.

POTATO OMELET

A delicate French invention to serve with ham or sausage.

2 medium potatoes, boiled
1 tablespoon butter
3 eggs

1 tablespoon water
½ cup grated cheese (Swiss, cheddar, Parmesan)

Slice boiled potatoes into ¼ inch slices. Place in skillet with melted butter. Combine eggs and water, beat lightly, and pour over potatoes. Cook omelet until set, then sprinkle with cheese and let cheese melt. Serve. Makes 1 omelet.

CURRIED POTATOES

Potatoes with an exotic touch to partner chicken or lamb.

3 medium potatoes
¼ cup butter
1 small onion, minced
½ cup chicken broth

1 or more teaspoons curry powder
1 tablespoon lemon juice
Salt and pepper to taste

Cube potatoes and cook until tender. Melt butter in skillet and sauté onion. Drain potatoes and add to onion. Cook, stirring, until potatoes become lightly colored. Add remaining ingredients and cook, stirring occasionally, until broth has evaporated. Serves 4-6.

POTATOES IN BEER

An Old World method that gives boiled potatoes a scrumptious taste and a lovely texture.

6 medium potatoes, quartered
3 cups beer

Salt and pepper
Butter

Place potatoes in large saucepan and pour in beer. There should be enough to come about ¾ of the way up the potatoes. Bring to boil and cook over moderate heat at a simmer for 15 minutes, until potatoes are tender. Drain and serve sprinkled with salt and pepper and dotted with butter. Serves 6-8.

CHEESE-TOPPED BROILED POTATOES

Cut into small rounds, these serve very well as hors d'oeuvres. Or keep the slices full-size and serve with any kind of roast.

4 medium potatoes
¼ cup butter
½ pound mozzarella cheese

Slice potatoes into slices ½ inch thick. Butter 1 side and broil until crispy brown. Turn, butter second side, and top with piece of cheese. Broil until cheese melts and becomes brown. Serves 4.

SUPER SLICES

The butter bakes right into potatoes cooked this way. Luscious.

4 medium potatoes
4 tablespoons butter
Salt and pepper to taste

Preheat oven to 375°F. Wash potatoes and cut into slices ¼ inch thick. Butter slices on both sides and sprinkle with salt and pepper. Lay in single layer on greased baking sheet. Cover with tinfoil and bake for 15 to 20 minutes, until tender. Turn once during baking. Serves 4.

LEMON POTATOES

Serve this lemony potato dish with baked fish.

6 medium potatoes, cut into chunks
1 medium onion, chopped
Grated rind and juice of 1 lemon
2 tablespoons flour

2 tablespoons butter
⅓ cup chopped fresh parsley
½ teaspoon ground nutmeg

Preheat oven to 450°F. Steam potatoes for 4 minutes, just to start them cooking. Combine with onion, lemon rind, flour, butter, parsley, and nutmeg and stir to coat potato chunks thoroughly. Place chunks in 1½-quart casserole, cover, and bake 15 to 20 minutes, until potatoes are barely tender. Squeeze lemon juice over chunks and serve. Serves 6-8.

POTATOES ROMANOFF

Rich and delicious. This can be eaten as a side dish or, with light salad, as a meal in itself.

4 medium potatoes, steamed and
  sliced
1 cup cottage cheese
1 cup sour cream or plain yogurt
1 cup grated Swiss or cheddar cheese

2 cups milk
1 tablespoon minced onion
⅛ teaspoon garlic powder
½ teaspoon salt
1 cup buttered bread crumbs

Preheat oven to 350°F. Combine all ingredients except bread crumbs and toss gently to combine thoroughly. Transfer to greased 1½-quart casserole and sprinkle top with crumbs. Bake 50 to 60 minutes, until top is brown and crusty. Serves 6-8 as side dish, 4 as main dish.

DUSTY POTATOES

The crumbs give a wonderfully crusty outside. Irresistible.

1½ cups dry bread crumbs
1 tablespoon nutmeg
1 teaspoon salt

½ teaspoon pepper
8 medium potatoes, quartered
½ cup melted butter

Preheat oven to 350°F. Combine bread crumbs, nutmeg, salt, and pepper. Dip potato quarters in butter, then roll them in seasoned crumbs. Place in greased baking pan and bake for 50 to 60 minutes, until outside is crisp and inside is tender. Serves 8.

POTATOES DAUPHINOIS

Scalloped potatoes with a French flair.

6 medium potatoes
½ teaspoon salt
½ teaspoon pepper

½ teaspoon nutmeg
4 tablespoons butter
1 cup light cream

Preheat oven to 350°F. Thinly slice potatoes. In greased 1½-quart baking dish, layer potatoes, seasonings, and 3 tablespoons butter in 3 stages. Pour cream over layers and dot with remaining butter. Bake 45 to 50 minutes, until cream has been absorbed and potatoes are tender. Serves 6.

POTATO NESTS

Fill these with salmon-in-cream sauce, or any creamed meat or vegetable for a decorative and delicious dish.

5 medium potatoes
3 tablespoons butter
Salt

Preheat oven to 450°F. Peel potatoes and cut into very thin strips. Fry in butter in skillet until almost tender, but do not brown. Remove from pan and sprinkle with salt. Distribute among 8 muffin cups, pressing against sides and bottom. Bake in oven about 15 minutes, until brown. Remove to plates, fill with creamed food, and serve. Serves 8.

SAXONY PUDDING

This slightly-sweet custardy pudding is traditionally eaten with a mug of fresh hot coffee close at hand.

3 medium potatoes
6 large prunes, pitted and chopped
3 slices bacon
2 cups milk
3 eggs, slightly beaten

½ cup flour
½ teaspoon salt
1 tablespoon sugar
Nutmeg

Preheat oven to 450°F. Grate potatoes and place in sieve to drain. Pit and chop prunes and fry bacon until crisp. Drain and crumble bacon. Combine potatoes, prunes and bacon and spread in bottom of greased 1½-quart deep baking dish or casserole. In separate bowl, combine milk, eggs, flour, salt, and sugar and blend until smooth. Pour carefully over potato mixture and dust top with nutmeg. Place in oven and cook at 450°F. for 10 minutes. Then turn oven to 350°F. and bake 20 to 30 minutes longer, until custard is firm and top is golden. Serves 4-6.

(Note: A few pieces of day-old roll can be set on top of custard as it goes into the oven. They will become moist and succulent and add a special touch to the pudding.)

Saucy Potatoes

CHEESE SAUCE FOR POTATOES

Pour this over hot boiled potatoes and serve with ham or egg dishes.

2 tablespoons butter
2 tablespoons flour
2 cups milk
½ teaspoon salt

¼ teaspoon pepper
½ cup grated Swiss, cheddar,
American, or Romano cheese
Minced pimiento or chopped parsley

Melt butter in heavy saucepan and stir in flour. Gradually stir in milk a little at a time to make a smooth mixture. Cook over low heat, stirring constantly, until sauce thickens. Stir in seasonings and grated cheese and stir until cheese melts completely. Pour sauce over hot potatoes, or stir potatoes into sauce and heat thoroughly. Garnish with pimiento or parsley. Enough sauce for 6 medium potatoes, or 12 small new potatoes.

CREAMED POTATOES

Add herbs (a pinch of tarragon, parsley, or chives) to this basic cream sauce to vary the flavor. Use sauce not only with cubed potatoes, as here, but over tender boiled new potatoes as well.

2 tablespoons butter
2 tablespoons flour
½ teaspoon salt
¼ teaspoon pepper

2 cups milk
1 teaspoon lemon juice
6 cooked potatoes, cubed
Chopped parsley

In large saucepan, melt butter. Stir in flour and seasonings. Slowly pour in milk, stirring constantly, and cook, stirring, until sauce thickens. Sprinkle lemon juice over cubed potatoes and add potatoes to cream sauce. Cook over low heat until potatoes are hot. Serve garnished with chopped parsley. Serves 6.

DONEGAL PIE

This Irish concoction makes a substantial breakfast or a hearty supper. Top with parsleyed cream sauce (see above) for complete authenticity.

8 medium potatoes, cooked and
    mashed, hot
Salt and pepper
2 hard-boiled eggs, sliced

2 slices bacon, fried until crisp and
    crumbled
Bacon fat from frying
Pastry for single crust

Preheat oven to 425°F. Grease a deep 8- or 9-inch pie plate. Spread half of potatoes in bottom and up sides. Cover this layer with sliced eggs, and top with bacon pieces. Drizzle hot bacon fat over pie. Cover layers with the remaining mashed potatoes. Roll out pastry to fit atop pie, cut decorative slits, and place on pie. Seal edges. Bake 20 to 25 minutes, or until nicely browned. Serve hot with hot cream sauce. Serves 6-8.

POTATOES IN FRUIT SAUCE

Serve this with roast duck or turkey for a fruitful treat. Peaches or mixed fruits can also be used in this recipe.

2 tablespoons butter
1 small onion, minced
2 tablespoons flour
1½ cups water
Brown sugar (¼ cup or to taste)

½ teaspoon salt
1 teaspoon cinnamon
½ teaspoon allspice
4 medium, firm pears or apples
6 medium potatoes

Melt butter in skillet and add onion and flour. Brown them and add water gradually, stirring constantly. Cook and stir until mixture is smooth and slightly thickened. Stir in sugar, salt and spices. Peel and core fruit and cut into quarters. Quarter potatoes. Place fruit and potatoes in sauce and spoon sauce over them. Cook over low heat, covered, until fruit and potatoes are tender, about 20 minutes. Serves 8-10.

POTATOES IN MUSTARD SAUCE

Marvelous served beside ham or corned beef.

8 medium potatoes
6 tablespoons butter
1 small onion, minced
3 tablespoons flour
1½ cups ham or beef broth

Salt and pepper
¼ cup prepared mustard
¼ cup bread crumbs or crushed
  potato chips

Boil potatoes, and drain. Cut into ½-inch slices. Arrange in circles in greased 9-inch pie plate. Melt 3 tablespoons butter in saucepan and sauté onion. Stir in flour, and slowly pour in broth, stirring constantly. Cook, stirring, until sauce thickens. Add salt and pepper to taste. Stir in mustard and pour over potatoes. Sprinkle top with bread crumbs or crushed potato chips and dot with last 3 tablespoons butter. Bake at 375°F. for 20 minutes. Serves 6-8.

POTATOES IN BARBECUE SAUCE

A real zesty flavor that is a natural with grilled franks.

1½ cups water
1 tablespoon wine vinegar
½ cup barbecue sauce
½ teaspoon salt

Pepper to taste
6 medium potatoes, sliced thin
1 medium onion, sliced thin

Preheat oven to 350°F. Combine water, vinegar, sauce, salt and pepper, and heat to boiling. Add potatoes and onion, stirring gently to mix with sauce. Pour into greased 1½-quart casserole, cover, and bake 50 to 60 minutes, until potatoes are nicely tender. Serve right away, good and hot, or chill and serve cold. Serves 6-8.

POTATOES WITH HOLLANDAISE

The fabled sauce enhances potatoes, too.

4 medium potatoes, cubed or sliced
1 cup chicken broth
½ cup butter
2 teaspoons lemon juice
3 egg yolks

4 tablespoons hot water
¼ teaspoon salt
Dash cayenne pepper
Chopped fresh parsley

Cook potatoes in broth until tender, about 15 minutes. Drain. Cream butter and beat lemon juice into it. In top of double boiler over hot water, beat egg yolks until thick. Beat in hot water one tablespoon at a time, allowing mixture to thicken after each addition. Remove from heat and beat in butter mixture. Beat in salt and cayenne. Spoon over hot potatoes and toss gently to mix. Place in serving dish and garnish with parsley. Serves 4.

CARAMEL POTATOES

The smallest and newest potatoes of the year are best for this.

12 small new potatoes
3 tablespoons sugar
3 tablespoons butter

Boil potatoes for 15 to 20 minutes, until tender. Gently remove skins. Spread sugar in skillet and heat slowly, stirring constantly, until sugar melts and turns brown. Stir in butter and blend well. Add potatoes and stir to coat evenly with caramel. Serves 4.

CHEESE-COATED POTATOES

New potatoes never tasted so good.

½ cup grated cheese
½ teaspoon salt
⅛ teaspoon pepper

12 small boiled new potatoes
¼ cup melted butter

Preheat oven to 400°F. Combine cheese, salt, and pepper. Roll hot potatoes first in butter, then in cheese mixture. Place on baking sheet and put in oven 10 to 15 minutes, until cheese melts and browns lightly. Serves 6.

SWISS-STYLE NEW POTATOES

Vary the cheese you grate over the top of this dish and take an imaginary tour of Europe.

12 small new potatoes
1½ cups grated Swiss or Gruyère
   cheese

Boil potatoes in water until barely tender. Drain, place in single layer in baking dish, and sprinkle with cheese. Bake in 350°F. oven until cheese just begins to melt, about 5 minutes. Serves 6.

POTATOES IN CASSEROLE WITH OTHER VEGETABLES, MEAT OR FISH

Combinations of potatoes with carrots, cabbage, tomatoes, spinach, in fact almost any other vegetable, are colorful and inviting. Of course, potatoes go with meat like blue goes with sky, but they are also deliciously compatible with fish and seafood.

Potato-Vegetable Casseroles

HUTSPOT

A Pennsylvania Dutch dish based on the contents of the root cellar.

6 medium onions, peeled
6 medium carrots, peeled
8 medium potatoes, peeled

Salt and pepper to taste
½ cup milk or light cream
3 tablespoons butter

Cut up onions and carrots and steam until tender (about 20 minutes). Drain. Cut up potatoes and steam them also — about 15 minutes. Drain and shake over low heat until completely dry. Combine three vegetables and mash to creamy smoothness. Season mixture and stir in milk or cream and butter. Pile in serving dish and present. Serves 8-10.

CARROT-POTATO CASSEROLE

A colorful combination that uses the same ingredients as the preceding recipe — but a different cooking method. Tastes good, too.

4 medium potatoes, sliced
1 medium onion, sliced
4 medium carrots, sliced

1 tablespoon butter
1 tablespoon flour
2 cups milk or light cream

Preheat oven to 350°F. Grease a 9-inch baking pan and spread potatoes, onions, and carrots in it in layers. In small saucepan, melt butter and stir in flour. Gradually pour in milk, stirring constantly, until mixture is thoroughly blended and smooth. Pour over vegetables. Cover with aluminum foil and bake 30 minutes. Uncover and bake 30 minutes longer, until vegetables are tender. Serves 6-8.

POTATOES AND BEANS IN SOUR CREAM

Peas, broccoli, Italian green beans, carrots, beets, limas, turnips, onions, or mushrooms, alone or in combination, are equally delicious in this sauce. Doubles as a salad, too.

3 medium potatoes, peeled and
  cubed
2 cups fresh green beans or other
  vegetable, rendered bite-sized
¾ cup sour cream

2 tablespoons cider vinegar
½ teaspoon salt
Dash pepper
¼ teaspoon sugar

Steam vegetables over boiling water until tender, about 10 minutes. Combine sour cream and remaining ingredients and stir in potatoes and beans. Allow to cool slightly and serve, or chill and serve as a salad. Serves 4-6.

PAPRIKA POTATO MEDLEY

Almost any vegetable, fresh, frozen, or leftover, can be used in this tasty dish. Here are the basics.

1 medium onion, sliced
1 tablespoon butter
1 medium potato, cubed
2 stalks celery, sliced in 1-inch pieces
2 or 3 vegetables (1 cup each) —
  corn, beans, peas, squash, limas,
  carrots, turnips

¾ teaspoon paprika
Pepper to taste
1 tablespoon cornstarch
½ cup water

Sauté onion in butter in heavy skillet until onion is tender. Add potato and celery, and sauté until lightly colored. Add remaining vegetables, paprika, and pepper. Cover and cook over low heat, stirring occasionally, until vegetables are done. In small cup, mix together cornstarch and water. Pour over vegetables and cook, stirring, until sauce thickens. Serves 6 or more, depending on number of vegetables included.

COLCANNON #1

The Irish affectionately call this dish and its variations using kale or spring onions Cally, Stelk, Champ, or Thump. Families bury a piece of money in the dish of Colcannon at Halloween and whoever finds it in his portion will have especially good luck.

1 onion, minced
1 tablespoon butter or bacon fat
6 medium potatoes, cooked and
  mashed

Salt and pepper
1½ cups green cabbage or kale, finely
  chopped and cooked

Sauté onion in butter or fat until tender, but do not brown. Combine with remaining ingredients and mix well. Put in lightly greased baking dish and heat in 350°F. oven 20 minutes, until good and hot, or heat over low heat on top of stove. Dot with butter and serve. Serves 6-8.

COLCANNON #2

Mashed leftover turnip is also a popular addition to either recipe.

6 medium potatoes, cooked,
  mashed, and chilled
Equal amount cold cooked cabbage

2 tablespoons melted butter
Salt and pepper
½ cup bread crumbs

Preheat oven to 350°F. Mash potatoes and beat until smooth. Chop cabbage and combine with potatoes. Add melted butter, salt and pepper, and mix thoroughly. Grease a 1½-quart baking dish and sprinkle bottom with half of bread crumbs. Fill with Colcannon and sprinkle remaining crumbs over top. Bake 25 to 30 minutes, until Colcannon is heated through and top is crusty. Serves 6-8.

POTATO-PARSNIP STEW

For a sublime flavor, let the vegetables get good and crusty before adding sauce. If parsnips are not available, turnips make a good substitute. Complete the meal with bratwurst and spinach salad.

4 medium potatoes
2 medium parsnips, or 1 medium
  turnip, peeled
5 tablespoons butter
1 large onion, coarsely chopped

Salt and pepper to taste
2 tablespoons flour
1½ cups broth
1 cup medium cream

Cube potatoes and parsnips or turnip. Melt 3 tablespoons butter in large skillet and sauté potatoes, onions, and parsnips until crusty and brown. Sprinkle with salt and pepper to taste. Meanwhile, melt 2 tablespoons butter in saucepan. Stir in flour and cook, stirring, until thoroughly combined. Slowly add broth, stirring constantly until sauce thickens. Strain, if desired, to remove any lumps. Stir this sauce into browned vegetables and heat gently almost to boiling. Just before serving, stir in cream. Serves 4-6.

POTATO-SPINACH CROQUETTES

An elegant vegetable course.

2 cups hot mashed potatoes
2 tablespoons butter
2 egg yolks, beaten slightly
½ cup cooked chopped spinach,
  drained

Salt and pepper to taste
1 egg, beaten slightly
1 cup dry bread crumbs
Fat for frying

Combine potatoes, butter, egg yolks, spinach, salt, and pepper. Blend thoroughly. Shape into 8 rectangles. Dip in beaten egg, then coat with bread crumbs. Fry in deep fat heated to 385°F. until crusty and brown, or fry in skillet, turning to brown both sides. Serves 4.

POTATO-TOMATO DISH

A nice accompaniment to roast chicken that cooks in the oven alongside the roast.

3 medium potatoes, sliced ½ inch thick

2 medium tomatoes, peeled and cut up

1 medium onion, sliced thin

Salt and pepper to taste

(½ teaspoon oregano)

1 tablespoon olive oil or melted butter

Preheat oven to 350°F. Place vegetables in greased 1½-quart casserole dish with salt, pepper, and optional oregano and drizzle oil or butter over them. Stir gently to coat vegetables. Cover and cook in oven for 30-40 minutes, until tomatoes have become good and juicy. Uncover and bake 30 minutes longer, until potatoes are tender. Serves 4-6.

Basically Stew

"THEN SOME" BEEF STEW

A "meat in potatoes" meal par excellence. Top with dumplings, if you like (p. 123 ff.).

2 pounds stewing beef, cubed

2 tablespoons flour

2 tablespoons butter

1 medium onion, chopped

2 cups water

1 16-ounce can tomatoes

½ cup red wine, Burgundy type

1 tablespoon Worcestershire sauce

1 teaspoon salt

Pepper to taste

1 clove garlic, crushed

4 medium potatoes, cubed

2 stalks celery, coarsely chopped

Coat meat with flour and brown evenly in butter. Remove to heavy stew pot. Sauté onions in butter until golden and add to meat. Pour in water and all other ingredients except potatoes and celery. Cover pot and bring to boil. Simmer, covered, 1 hour, or until meat is tender. Add potatoes and celery, cover again, and simmer ½ hour longer. Adjust seasonings and serve. Serves 8.

PERUVIAN BEEF STEW

Spicy and satisfying.

2 cloves garlic, crushed
2 tablespoons cooking oil
1 medium tomato
1 medium onion, finely chopped
1 teaspoon cayenne or ground red
  chili
Salt and pepper to taste
1 teaspoon oregano

1 teaspoon finely chopped fresh mint
  leaves
1 pound stewing beef, cut into
  chunks
1 quart water
2 tablespoons rice
3 medium potatoes
1 tablespoon vinegar

Brown crushed garlic in oil. Peel tomato, chop, and add it to pot. Add onion, seasonings, and herbs and cook until onion is tender. Add meat cubes and cook until brown on all sides. Pour in water and add rice. Cook, covered, over medium to low heat for 45 minutes, until meat is about half cooked. Peel and quarter potatoes and add them to pot. Continue cooking covered pot over low heat another 45 minutes until potatoes are done. Perk flavor with vinegar and serve. Serves 4.

CORNED BEEF AND CABBAGE

The traditional St. Patrick's Day dinner. Serve with horseradish sauce.

4 pounds corned beef, round or
  brisket
Water
1 bay leaf
4 medium onions, quartered

4 medium carrots, cut into 1-inch
  pieces
4 medium potatoes, quartered
1 large head cabbage, cut into wedges

Place corned beef in large pot or kettle and add water to cover. Add bay leaf, cover, and simmer 3 to 4 hours, until meat is tender. Pour off water. To drained beef, add 2 cups fresh water, onions, carrots, and potatoes. Cover and simmer 20 minutes, until potatoes are almost tender. Add cabbage wedges, cover, and cook another 10 to 15 minutes, until cabbage is done. Serves 6-8.

REAL RED FLANNEL HASH

A wonderful way with leftover corned beef.

2 tablespoons butter or bacon fat
6 medium beets, cooked, peeled and
  chopped
4 medium potatoes, steamed and
  diced

2 cups chopped cooked corned beef
2 tablespoons cream

Combine butter or fat, beets, potatoes, and beef in skillet. Moisten with a little water and cover. Cook over low heat until meat is crisp and brown. At last minute, stir in cream, let heat, and serve. Serves 4.

POTATOES AND VEAL ITALIAN

The subtle flavor of this Italian-style stew is molto bene — *even* benissimo!

8 pieces veal shank
1 to 2 tablespoons cooking oil,
  preferably olive oil
1 medium onion, sliced
1 clove garlic, crushed
¾ cup white wine
2 tablespoons tomato paste
1 tablespoon lemon juice
1 cup water or chicken broth
2 teaspoons oregano

1 teaspoon thyme
½ teaspoon rosemary
1 bay leaf
4 medium potatoes, quartered
8 small white onions
4 medium carrots, sliced into ½-inch
  rounds
2 stalks celery, sliced into ½-inch
  rounds
Salt and pepper to taste

Sauté veal in oil in heavy stew pot until meat is brown on both sides. Sauté sliced onion and garlic until lightly browned. Add wine, tomato paste, lemon juice, water or broth, and herbs. Stir gently to blend. Cover pot, bring to boil, and simmer about 1 hour, or until meat is barely tender. Add vegetables, cover, and simmer 30 to 40 minutes longer, until vegetables are tender. Salt and pepper to taste. Top with dumplings (p. 123 ff.) during last few minutes of cooking, if desired. Serves 6-8.

SPRINGTIME LAMB STEW

This stew is best made with the earliest, tenderest spring vegetables.

2½ pounds stewing lamb, cut in
  chunks
10 small onions
4 tablespoons butter
1 cup water
2 whole tomatoes, peeled and
  chopped, or ¾ cup tomato juice
1 tablespoon chopped fresh dill weed
  or 2 teaspoons dried

Salt and pepper to taste
10 small new potatoes, unpeeled
10 baby carrots, halved
½ pound fresh young green beans, or
  1 10-ounce package frozen
  French-style

Sauté lamb chunks and onions in butter in heavy pot until brown. Drain off any excess fat. Pour in water, add tomatoes or juice, dill, salt, and pepper. Cover pot and simmer over low heat about 1 hour, until lamb is barely tender. Add potatoes and carrots and cook 30 to 40 minutes longer, until potatoes are tender. Add green beans and cook another 5 to 10 minutes, until beans are still slightly crisp. Serves 8-10.

GERMAN POTATO STEW

Serve with slabs of pumpernickel or black bread and hot beets.

½ pound pork sausage
3 medium potatoes, sliced ½ inch
thick
2 tablespoons flour
2 cups boiling water

1½ teaspoons vinegar
1 small head cabbage, cut into
wedges
1 tablespoon caraway seed
1 cup sour cream

In skillet, cook sausage until browned. Drain off all but 2 tablespoons fat and
add potatoes. Sprinkle with flour. Combine boiling water and vinegar and
pour in. Cover and cook over medium heat 15 minutes, until potatoes are
tender. Lay cabbage wedges on top, sprinkle with caraway seeds, cover, and
cook 10 minutes longer, until cabbage is done. Serve topped with dollops of
sour cream. Serves 4.

ORIENTAL STIR-FRIED POTATOES

*Augment this Far-Eastern dish with mushrooms, water chestnuts, bamboo shoots,
and/or snow peas as desired.*

3 medium potatoes, cooked until still
slightly firm
2 tablespoons cooking oil
1 cup diced cooked beef, pork, or
chicken
2 scallions, including green tops,
chopped

3 tablespoons dry white wine or
vermouth
½ teaspoon salt
½ teaspoon ginger
1 tablespoon soy sauce

Dice potatoes. Heat oil in large heavy frying pan or wok. Add potatoes, meat,
and scallions, and cook, stirring, until meat is brown and scallions wilt
slightly. Stir in remaining ingredients and continue to cook and stir until
mixture is good and hot. Serves 2-3.

Meat 'n Potatoes

SHEPHERD'S PIE

*Shepherds used lamb in this dish, but pork, beef, or chicken taste equally good.
This version has a real (potato) crust.*

Filling:
3 tablespoons butter or fat
1 cup cubed cooked meat
3 medium onions, sliced
1 cup gravy

2 cups cooked vegetables (carrots,
peas, beans, corn, limas)
Salt and pepper to taste

Melt butter and brown meat in it. Stir in remaining ingredients and heat
through.

Crust:

1 cup hot mashed potatoes
¼ teaspoon salt
1 teaspoon baking powder

1 egg, beaten
2 tablespoons melted butter
2 tablespoons flour

Combine ingredients and blend thoroughly. Roll out to ¼-inch thickness on lightly floured board.

Preheat oven to 350°F. Place filling in 1½-quart baking dish. Cover carefully with crust, and prick crust decoratively to let steam escape. Bake 30 minutes, or until brown. Serves 6.

PIZZA ON POTATOES

Believe it or not, seasoned mashed potatoes make a terrific base for pizza. Add your favorite ingredients — sausage, mushrooms, or whatever — to this basic recipe.

Crust:

4 cups mashed potatoes
½ cup flour
2 tablespoons minced or grated
  onion

1 egg
1 clove garlic, crushed
2 tablespoons melted butter
1 teaspoon oregano

Preheat oven to 375°F. Combine ingredients and blend thoroughly. Spread on greased pizza pan or on greased cookie sheet, making a ridge around the edge.

Sauce:

2 cups tomatoes, crushed, or tomato
  puree
3 tablespoons tomato paste
1 teaspoon oregano
1 clove garlic, crushed

1 small onion, minced
Salt and pepper to taste
1 teaspoon basil
6 ounces grated mozzarella cheese

Combine ingredients except cheese over medium heat and simmer 15 minutes. Spoon onto crust. Top with grated cheese and your favorite pizza stuff — sausage, ground beef, mushrooms, anchovies, green pepper, pepperoni, or whatever. Bake 20-25 minutes, until crust is nice and brown and cheese has melted. Serve on plates. Serves 4-6.

POTATO-BASE HAM AND CHEESE PIE

Superb down-home fare fancy enough to appear at the toniest brunch, this is first cousin to a French quiche.

Crust:
2 cups mashed potatoes
2 tablespoons prepared mustard

Combine potatoes and mustard and spread evenly in bottom of greased 9-inch pie pan.

Filling:

1 pound cooked ham, diced	3 eggs, beaten
1 small onion, chopped	½ cup grated Swiss or cheddar cheese
1 teaspoon butter	1½ cups milk or light cream

Preheat oven to 350°F. Sprinkle ham over potato crust. Sauté onion in butter and sprinkle over ham. Combine remaining ingredients and pour over pie. Bake 30 to 40 minutes, until filling is set and lightly browned. Serves 4-6.

COUNTRY PIE

German farmers enjoy this after a morning's work in the field.

½ pound pork sausage	½ teaspoon horseradish
2 teaspoons caraway seed	3 cups hot seasoned mashed potatoes
2 cups sauerkraut, drained	2 tablespoons butter

Preheat oven to 350°F. Place sausage in bottom of greased 1½-quart baking dish. Stir caraway seed into sauerkraut and add to sausage. Stir horseradish into mashed potatoes and spread over sausage mixture. Dot top with butter. Bake 30-40 minutes, until sausage is done and top is crusty. Serves 4-6.

DUBLIN CODDLE

Traditionally made with lean bacon and the finest pork sausage, and eaten right from the pot. Chunks of brown bread soak up what's left.

¼ pound lean bacon, cut up	½ pound lean pork sausages
1 large onion, sliced	Water (or half water and half milk)
4 large potatoes, sliced	Fresh parsley sprigs

Fry bacon until almost crisp. In greased skillet or 1½-quart casserole, place bacon, onion, and potatoes in layers. Top with sausages. Add water, or half water and half milk, to cover. Cover skillet or casserole and simmer on top of stove for 1 hour, or bake for 1 hour at 350°F. Or, if more convenient, bake this at very low heat (300°F.), and it will keep warm for hours. Garnish with parsley and serve piping hot. Serves 4-6.

LANCASTER COUNTY POTATOES AND FRANKS

A favorite in Pennsylvania Dutch country.

6 medium potatoes, peeled,
  steamed, and sliced or diced
2 scallions, chopped, including green
  part
2 tablespoons bacon fat or butter
6 large frankfurters or knackwurst,
  sliced into ½-inch rounds

1 tablespoon sugar
2 teaspoons flour
½ teaspoon salt
⅓ cup vinegar
½ cup water
1 tablespoon chopped fresh parsley

Peel and dice potatoes while hot and keep them warm in oven-proof serving dish. Sauté scallions in bacon fat or butter and add to potatoes. Brown franks or knackwurst in fat and add rounds to potatoes and onions. Stir sugar, flour, and salt into drippings in pan. When mixture bubbles, gradually stir in vinegar and water and cook, stirring, until mixture thickens. Pour hot sauce over potato mixture, garnish with parsley, and serve. Serves 6.

POTATO-APPLE PORK CHOPS

This recipe was brought to America by Danish settlers.

6 pork chops, ½ to ¾ inch thick
1 medium onion, sliced thin
1 teaspoon curry
Salt and pepper to taste
2 cups chicken broth or water

2 medium potatoes, sliced ¼ inch
  thick
1 large tart apple, coarsely chopped
1 tablespoon lemon juice
(2 teaspoons brown sugar)

Brown chops on both sides in large cast-iron frying pan. Add onions and brown lightly. Add seasonings, broth or water, and potatoes, spreading potatoes over chops. Cover and simmer over low heat 30 to 45 minutes, until chops are barely tender. Add chopped apple and lemon juice, cover, and simmer 15 minutes longer. Just before serving, sprinkle with optional brown sugar. Serves 6.

SCALLOPED POTATOES WITH HAM

A nifty way to re-present ham; works well with ham steak, too.

8 medium potatoes, peeled and
    sliced ¼ inch thick
2 tablespoons flour
1 small onion, chopped
½ teaspoon salt

Pepper
2 cups milk
1 cup grated cheese, Swiss or
    cheddar
Ham slices or 1-inch ham steak

Preheat oven to 350°F. In greased 2½-quart casserole, lay ⅓ of the potatoes, sprinkle with flour, onion, and seasonings, and if you use sliced ham add a layer of ham slices. Repeat layers, ending with last third of potato slices. Pour milk over all. Sprinkle with grated cheese. If you use the ham steak, lay on top of potatoes, flour, onion, and seasonings. Again, pour over milk, and top with cheese. Bake 1¼ hours, until potatoes are tender and sauce has thickened slightly. Serves 8.

Variation:
Add layers of corn niblets, fresh, frozen, or canned and drained between those of potato and ham. Or if you use ham steak, layer corn and potatoes, and top with ham, milk, and cheese, as above.

PEELY SAUSAGE

Unique, nourishing, and fetching. Quantities depend on number to be served (see below).

Potato peelings
Sausage — (Country-style, German,
    Italian, Polish, any kind will do) —
    meat or links, cut into ½-inch
    pieces

Chopped onion
Grated cheese

Fry everything up together until sausage is done, peels are nicely browned, and onion is brown also. Sprinkle top with grated cheese, (use a mild cheese with a strong sausage, a strong cheese with a mild sausage), and serve. Great with eggs for breakfast, or with green salad for supper. Allow peelings from 2 potatoes, ¼ onion, ½ pound sausage, and ¼ cup grated cheese per person.

Some Things Fishy

CODFISH BALLS WITH TOMATO SAUCE

A breakfast tradition in New England. Good with baked beans for brunch, too.

½ pound salt cod
Cold water
2½ cups diced raw potatoes
1½ tablespoons butter or bacon fat

Dash pepper
2 tablespoons flour
1 egg, slightly beaten
Fat for deep frying

Soak salt cod in water 12 hours to remove excess salt, changing water 3 or 4 times. Pour off water. Flake cod with fork. Steam potatoes 10 minutes, drain, and shake over low heat until all water has evaporated and potatoes are mealy. Mash, add butter or fat, pepper, and flour, and beat until light. Beat in cod and egg and beat until mixture is fluffy. Drop by large spoonfuls into deep fat heated to 385°F. and fry until brown. Drain and serve with Tomato Sauce (see below). Serves 4.

Tomato Sauce:

2½ cups canned tomatoes and juice
1 small onion, chopped
½ teaspoon ground cloves
2 tablespoons butter

1 tablespoon flour
½ teaspoon salt
Dash pepper

Combine tomatoes, onion, and cloves and cook over medium heat for 10 minutes. Melt butter in small saucepan and stir in flour, salt, and pepper. Slowly stir in tomato mixture and cook, stirring, until sauce bubbles and thickens. Ladle over hot codfish balls.

POTATO CLAM PIE

Sunday brunch or supper are perfect occasions to serve potato clam pie.

4 cups sliced cooked potatoes
6 scallions, chopped
1 tablespoon butter
¼ teaspoon salt
Dash pepper
½ cup chopped celery

2 cups minced clams
1 cup milk
2 tablespoons sherry
1 tablespoon cornstarch
Baking-powder-biscuit dough

Preheat oven to 400°F. Combine all ingredients except dough and stir to blend well. Pour into deep greased 1½-quart baking dish. Roll out biscuit dough and cut to fit dish or into round biscuits. Place dough over potato-clam filling. Bake for 30 to 40 minutes, or until biscuits are done and filling is piping hot. Serves 6.

AMERICAN KEDGEREE

Often served for breakfast in great English country houses during the 19th and early 20th centuries. Originally made with rice, this is a tasty dish rendered even more substantial if you add kidney beans. Serve with a green salad for a delightful dinner, or omit beans and serve for brunch.

1 medium onion, chopped
4 tablespoons butter
1-pound can salmon, drained, boned, and flaked, or 2-3 cups leftover cooked fish, flaked
2 cups peeled, cooked, and riced potatoes

1 teaspoon lemon juice or vinegar
2 teaspoons curry powder, or to taste
Salt and pepper to taste
2 hard-boiled eggs, yolks and whites separated
(2 cups cooked kidney beans)
1 cup sour cream

Sauté onion in butter until lightly browned. Mix fish with potatoes. Add onion. Stir in lemon juice or vinegar and seasonings. Chop egg whites and add to fish mixture with optional kidney beans. Heat mixture until piping hot, stir in sour cream, place in serving dish, and top with grated egg yolks. Serves 6-8.

SALMON LOAF

A pretty and luxurious loaf.

2 cans (7¾ ounces each) salmon, drained, or 1 pound cooked fresh salmon
2 eggs, beaten
1 cup mashed potatoes
1 tablespoon minced onion

1 tablespoon chopped fresh dill
½ tablespoon lemon juice
Dash Worcestershire sauce, or ½ teaspoon grated horseradish
½ teaspoon salt
Pepper to taste

Preheat oven to 375°F. Combine all ingredients and blend well. Place in greased 8x4-inch loaf pan, or mound in greased baking dish, or place in 4 or 6 individual greased baking dishes. Bake loaf or mound 40 minutes; individual dishes 20 minutes. Drape with lemon-flavored cream sauce and serve. Serves 4-6.

DILLY SHRIMP AND POTATOES

Serve hot or cold for a light summer meal. Lamb substituted for shrimp makes an equally delicious dish; season with rosemary instead of dill.

3 medium potatoes
¼ cup minced onion
2 tablespoons butter
1 tablespoon flour
1 cup milk or light cream
½ teaspoon salt
Dash pepper
2 tablespoons sour cream

1 tablespoon fresh chopped dill weed, or ½ teaspoon dried, or, for lamb, ½ teaspoon dried rosemary
½ pound shelled and cooked shrimp, or 1 cup cooked diced lamb
Minced dill weed (or rosemary) for garnish

Cook potatoes until soft but still firm, about 10 minutes. Drain and keep hot. Sauté onion in butter and stir in flour. Slowly stir in milk and heat, stirring constantly, until mixture boils and thickens. Remove from heat and stir in seasonings and sour cream. Peel and dice potatoes and add with dill and shrimp to hot sauce. Cook over low heat until thoroughly heated, or place in refrigerator until thoroughly chilled. Sprinkle with more dill (or rosemary) and serve. Serves 4.

POTATO SALADS

Almost everyone likes the ubiquitous potato salad, and almost everyone has a definite opinion about it, even those who won't touch other salads. Make a universally acclaimed potato salad, and your success as a cook is assured. Some like 'em cold, and some like 'em hot, the preference often depending on the individual's upbringing or heritage. It is our hope that this chapter will provide at least one potato salad that's *right* for enthusiasts of every kind. Read on and explore. They're all good!

Cold Potato Salads

BASIC COLD POTATO SALAD

Deliciously simple this way, but embellish with any of the suggestions on p. 103.

4 medium potatoes
2 tablespoons minced onion
½ cup chopped celery

½ cup mayonnaise
1 teaspoon prepared mustard
Salt and pepper to taste

Boil potatoes, drain, and cut into cubes. Combine with onion and celery. Stir in mayonnaise, mustard, and salt and pepper. Chill 1 hour or longer. Serves 4.

BEETEN POTATO SALAD

Beautiful and Beety-full.

1 10-ounce can or jar pickled beets, and liquid
1 tablespoon Worcestershire sauce
1 tablespoon finely chopped onion
6 medium potatoes, cooked and sliced

Drain liquid from beets (reserve beets) and combine liquid with Worcestershire sauce and onion. Pour over sliced potatoes and stir gently to blend. Slice beets, if not already sliced, and spread over potatoes. Chill 2 or 3 hours. Just before serving, toss gently to mix beets and potatoes. Serves 6-8.

THINGS TO ADD TO POTATO SALAD

All of the ingredients below are good in cold potato salad, and many can be combined, according to taste.

Anchovies
Bacon, crumbled, or bacon-flavored bits
Capers
Carrot, raw, grated
Celery, raw, chopped
Chives, chopped
Chowchow
Cucumber, diced
Egg, hard-boiled, sliced or chopped
Green pepper, chopped
Ham or luncheon meat, chopped
Kidney or lima beans
Mushrooms, canned or fresh
Nuts, broken or chopped — pecans, walnuts, almonds, peanuts

Olives, ripe or stuffed, sliced
Onion, red or white, chopped or sliced
Peas
Pickled beets, sliced or chopped
Pickles, dill, chopped
Pickles, sweet, chopped
Pimiento
Red pepper, sweet, chopped
Relish, cucumber or corn
Tomatoes
Turkey or chicken, diced
Water chestnuts, chopped or sliced

CURRIED POTATO SALAD

Great with grilled spareribs, also barbecued or baked chicken.

3 medium potatoes, diced
1 tablespoon butter
1 small onion, chopped
1½ teaspoons curry powder
¼ teaspoon powdered ginger
¼ teaspoon ground allspice

1½ teaspoons grated orange rind
⅛ teaspoon cayenne pepper
1 tablespoon chopped parsley
⅓ cup currants
½ teaspoon salt
1 cup plain yogurt

Boil potatoes until barely tender, about 10 minutes. Drain. Melt butter in skillet and sauté onion until lightly browned. Stir in spices, orange rind, and pepper and remove from heat. Add potatoes and stir to coat with mixture. Stir in parsley. In separate bowl, combine currants, salt, and yogurt, and pour over potato mixture. Toss gently to blend. Transfer salad to bowl and chill thoroughly before serving. Serves 4-6.

GREAT GREEN POTATO SALAD

Perfect for a light luncheon.

6 medium potatoes, cooked
½ cup chopped celery
¼ cup chopped onion
1 tablespoon blue-cheese salad
    dressing

1 cup plain yogurt
½ cup buttermilk
Fresh parsley

Cube potatoes while hot and gently stir in celery and onion. Combine salad dressing, yogurt, and buttermilk in separate bowl and pour over potatoes. Mix gently. Chill, covered, until thoroughly cold. Serve with more blue cheese dressing, and garnish with parsley. Serves 6-8.

ITALIAN POTATO SALAD

You don't have to be Italian to like this one!

4 medium potatoes, cooked and
    cubed
4 ripe olives, pitted and sliced
1 egg

¼ cup Italian dressing
¼ cup grated Romano cheese
2 teaspoons Worcestershire sauce
2 teaspoons prepared mustard

Combine potatoes and olives in large bowl. Stir to blend. In separate bowl, beat together remaining ingredients. Pour over potato mixture and stir to blend. Chill and serve. Serves 4.

MASHED POTATO SALAD

Eye-catching served on tomato wedges, or inside tomato shells.

3 cups mashed potatoes
¼ cup French dressing
1 tablespoon chopped onion
2 tablespoons finely chopped celery

2 tablespoons finely chopped green
   pepper
2 hard-boiled eggs, chopped
¼ cup mayonnaise

Combine all ingredients and stir to blend thoroughly. Chill, and serve on or
in tomatoes. Serves 4-6.

NORTHERN MAINE POTATO SALAD

Colorful as well as tasty.

5 medium potatoes
Garlic powder
1 medium onion, chopped
¼ cup chopped cucumber
2 tablespoons chopped green pepper
1 tablespoon chopped sweet red
   pepper

2 tablespoons chopped fresh parsley,
   or 2 teaspoons dried
Salt and pepper to taste
French dressing
½ cup mayonnaise

Boil potatoes, peeled or unpeeled, and slice or dice them. Sprinkle sparingly
with garlic powder. In salad bowl, combine potatoes, vegetables, parsley and
seasonings. Pour in enough French dressing to coat salad lightly and toss.
Cover and chill for 8 hours or overnight. Just before serving, refresh salad
with mayonnaise and again toss gently. Serves 6.

PEACHY POTATO SALAD

*The combination sounds odd, but the result is sensational. Serve as part of a cool
summer repast.*

Salad:

4 small new potatoes, diced
1 medium carrot, diced
1 cup green beans, cut into ½-inch
   pieces

½ cup fresh peas
2 medium peaches, peeled and
   cubed, sprinkled with 1 tablespoon
   lemon juice

Cook vegetables separately in lightly salted water until barely tender, drain,
then dunk in cold water to stop cooking process and keep vegetables crisp.
Sprinkle peaches with lemon juice and combine with vegetables.

Dressing:

½ cup mayonnaise
2 tablespoons sour cream or yogurt
1 teaspoon spicy prepared mustard

2 tablespoons fresh chopped chives
½ teaspoon salt
Pepper to taste

Combine dressing ingredients, then add to salad. Toss gently to blend, cover,
and place in refrigerator to chill before serving. Serves 4.

PICKLED POTATO SALAD

Superb with pumpernickel-and-pastrami sandwiches.

4 cups diced cooked potatoes
2 tablespoons minced onion
4 sweet cucumber pickles, thinly
  sliced
½ fresh cucumber, thinly sliced
4 radishes, thinly sliced

½ teaspoon salt
Dash cayenne pepper
½ teaspoon dry mustard
¼ teaspoon pepper
Sour Cream Dressing (see below)
Parsley

Combine ingredients and stir in dressing (below). Chill until ready to serve, and garnish with parsley and more cucumber pickles, if desired. Serves 8.

Sour Cream Dressing:
1 teaspoon dry mustard
1 tablespoon sugar
½ teaspoon salt
¼ teaspoon pepper
2 tablespoons flour
½ cup water

2 egg yolks
¼ cup tarragon vinegar
2 tablespoons butter
1 cup sour cream, whipped (or use
  plain yogurt)

Combine first five ingredients and stir into water until smooth. In top of double boiler combine egg yolks and vinegar. Beat until light and lemon-colored. Beat in first mixture. Cook, stirring, over hot water until mixture thickens. Stir in butter until melted. Chill mixture thoroughly. When ready to use, stir in sour cream. Makes about 2 cups dressing.

POTATO AND MUSHROOM SALAD

A really delectable combination.

½ cup olive oil
1 clove garlic, crushed
Salt and pepper to taste
1 teaspoon dried oregano
1 teaspoon dried basil
½ teaspoon sugar

4 medium potatoes, cooked and
  sliced
¼ pound chopped fresh mushrooms,
  or 1 6-ounce can, with liquid
¼ cup water for fresh mushrooms

Combine olive oil, garlic, salt and pepper, oregano, basil, and sugar. Pour over potatoes and stir gently to coat all slices. Boil mushrooms in water or canning liquid and cook until tender. Pour mushrooms and liquid over potatoes, stir gently, and chill thoroughly. Serves 4-6.

RAINBOW POTATO SALAD

A festive salad alight with color and taste.

2 cups cooked cubed potatoes
1 cup cooked baby lima beans
½ cup chopped celery
⅓ cup grated raw carrots
⅓ cup cubed cooked beets

4 hard-boiled eggs, sliced
½ cup minced shallots or chives
Salt and pepper to taste
¾ cup French dressing
¼-½ cup mayonnaise

Combine all ingredients except mayonnaise and stir gently to mix. Marinate in refrigerator one hour or longer. At serving time, stir in enough mayonnaise to moisten. Serves 4-6.

SALADE NICOISE

French in origin, but international in appeal.

8 medium potatoes, cooked and
   diced
4 hard-boiled eggs, sliced
1 small can anchovies, drained and
   chopped
⅓ cup capers
2 medium tomatoes, seeded and
   diced

2 small onions, sliced
2 cups whole cooked green beans
Oil-and-vinegar French dressing
2 teaspoons oregano
½ cup pitted and halved ripe olives
¼ cup chopped pimiento

In large bowl, combine all ingredients except olives and pimiento and stir gently to blend. Or layer ingredients and pour combined dressing ingredients over all. Garnish with olives and pimiento. Chill and serve. Serves 8-10.

SALAD IN POTATOES

Wherein potato skins are used as a container for salad or other filling.

6 medium potatoes
½ cup French dressing

Boil potatoes, unpeeled, until barely tender — about 15 minutes. Drain, cool, and peel if desired. Cut a slice from the bottom of each potato so it will sit upright. Carefully scoop out center of each potato, leaving a shell. Reserve potato pulp for another use. Drizzle dressing over shells and refrigerate 2 hours. Drain off any dressing. Fill cavities with vegetable, meat, fish, or potato salad, and serve. Serves 6.

SAVORY POTATO SALAD

Terrific with barbecued chicken.

Salad:

4 cups diced cooked potatoes
½ cup chopped celery
¼ cup chopped onion
¼ cup thinly sliced radishes
1 teaspoon celery seed

½ teaspoon salt
Pepper to taste
2 hard-boiled eggs, slices or
   wedges

In salad bowl, mix all but last ingredient together. Pour dressing (below) over vegetables and toss lightly to blend. Garnish with egg slices or wedges. Serves 8-10.

Dressing:

1 cup sour cream or plain yogurt
2 tablespoons lemon juice

2 teaspoons prepared mustard
1 teaspoon curry powder

Combine sour cream or yogurt, lemon juice, mustard, and curry powder and mix well.

SPINACH SALAD WITH POTATO DRESSING

Here's a switch, and a darned good one, too.

⅓ cup mashed potatoes
½ cup French dressing
Salt and pepper to taste

1 pound spinach, washed and dried
3 slices bacon
2 hard-boiled eggs, chopped

Combine potatoes, dressing, salt and pepper, and beat until smooth. Tear spinach leaves and pile in salad bowl. Fry bacon slices, drain, and crumble over spinach. Pour in fat from pan. Add eggs. Pour in potato-dressing mixture and toss. Serves 4-6.

RUSSIAN POTATO SALAD

Best with new potatoes.

6 medium new potatoes
⅓ cup grated onion
½ teaspoon celery seed
½ teaspoon salt
2 teaspoons sugar
Pepper

½ cup (approx.) Russian dressing
⅓ cup mayonnaise
1 tablespoon vinegar
9 medium radishes, diced
2 cups chopped celery

Boil potatoes, drain, and cube. While still warm, sprinkle with onion, celery seed, salt, sugar, and pepper. Combine dressing, mayonnaise, and vinegar, and stir into potatoes. Chill until ready to serve — at least 2 hours. Just before serving, add radishes and celery and toss salad lightly to blend. Add more Russian dressing if necessary. Serves 4-6.

WINED POTATO SALAD

A good springtime salad.

8 small new potatoes, boiled and sliced (peel if desired)
½ cup Sauterne or Rhine wine
3 scallions, sliced (including tops)
¼ cup salad oil

3 tablespoons tarragon vinegar
2 teaspoons sugar
Salt and pepper to taste
3 tablespoons chopped fresh parsley

While potatoes are still warm, pour wine over them. Stir in other ingredients gently, and chill well before serving. Serves 4-6.

MEAT AND POTATO MOLDED SALAD

Quintessential combination in a new guise.

Meat Layer:

1 envelope unflavored gelatin softened in ¼ cup cold water
1 12-ounce can luncheon meat, chopped
1 small onion, minced

½ cup mayonnaise
½ cup catsup
1 teaspoon horseradish
1 teaspoon prepared mustard

Dissolve gelatin over boiling water. Combine all ingredients and blend well. Lightly oil a 1½-quart mold and pour meat mixture into it. Chill until firm.

Potato Layer:

1 envelope unflavored gelatin softened in ¼ cup cold water
2 cups diced cooked potatoes
1 cup diced celery
1 small onion, minced
2 tablespoons finely chopped green pepper
½ cup mayonnaise

2 tablespoons milk
1 teaspoon salt
Pepper to taste
1 teaspoon prepared mustard
Lettuce
Tomato wedges
Devilled eggs

Dissolve gelatin over boiling water. Combine all ingredients except lettuce, tomato, and eggs, and blend well. When meat mixture is firm, spoon potato mixture on top of it and spread evenly. Chill until firm. Unmold on platter, garnish with lettuce leaves, tomato wedges, and devilled eggs. Serves 6.

BEEF PICNIC SALAD

A whole-meal salad with a gourmet touch.

1 pound cooked beef, trimmed of fat
3 tablespoons wine vinegar
2 tablespoons sherry, dry or sweet
1 tablespoon catsup
1 teaspoon prepared mustard

2 medium potatoes, cooked and
  cubed
¼ cup sliced, fresh mushrooms, or
  1 2-ounce can, drained
¼ cup sour cream

Cube beef into bite-size pieces. Combine beef with vinegar, sherry, catsup, and mustard. Place mixture in refrigerator for 2 or 3 hours to blend flavors. Stir occasionally. Then mix in potatoes, mushrooms, and sour cream. Chill and serve. Serves 4.

POTATO AND HERRING SALAD

This one comes straight from Scandinavia.

4 medium potatoes, cooked and
  cubed
1½ cups marinated herring fillets,
  cubed
¾ cup chopped celery

1 tablespoon chopped fresh parsley
1 tablespoon chopped fresh chives
½ cup sour cream
2 tablespoons lemon juice
Paprika

Combine ingredients in large bowl, toss lightly to mix, and serve. Serves 4-6.

POTATO/SAUSAGE SALAD

Another great main-dish potato salad, this one with a European flair.

4 cups cooked cubed potatoes
2 cups cubed hard salami or cooked
  Polish sausage
1 cup chopped celery
1 pimiento, diced
6 medium pickles, sweet or dill,
  diced

2 hard-boiled eggs, sliced
½ teaspoon salt
¾ cup mayonnaise
Lettuce
Tomato wedges
Cubed Swiss cheese

Combine all ingredients except lettuce, tomato, and cheese, and blend well. Serve on a bed of lettuce and garnish with tomato and cheese. Serves 6-8.

Hot Potato Salads

GERMAN HOT POTATO SALAD

The traditional and original hot potato salad. Or so some say.

4 slices bacon, chopped
¼ cup chopped onion
¼ cup chopped celery

1 medium dill pickle, chopped
6 medium potatoes, cooked and
  sliced

Fry bacon bits in skillet until crisp. Remove and reserve bacon bits. Add onion, celery, and pickle to bacon fat and cook until nicely tender. Add to potatoes with bacon bits. Pour dressing (below) over potato mixture, toss gently, and serve. Serves 6-8.

Dressing:
¼ cup water
½ cup vinegar
½ teaspoon sugar

¼ teaspoon salt
Dash paprika
¼ teaspoon dry mustard

In a small saucepan, combine dressing ingredients, stir until smooth, and heat to boiling. Pour dressing into skillet and stir to combine.

OREGANO POTATO SALAD

Make the dressing while the potatoes cook so the onions have plenty of time to blend with the other ingredients.

8 medium potatoes

Boil or steam potatoes until tender, about 20-25 minutes. Peel and cube while hot. Make dressing (below). Pour dressing over hot potatoes, stir gently to mix, and serve warm. Serves 6-8.

Dressing:
1 medium onion, minced
½ cup olive or other salad oil
Juice of 2 lemons
½ teaspoon salt

Pepper to taste
1 tablespoon oregano
½ teaspoon sugar

Combine dressing ingredients and let stand at room temperature at least 15 minutes.

SAUCY HOT POTATO SALAD

This snappy hot salad is a piquant variation on a favorite theme.

8 medium potatoes, cooked and
  peeled (if desired)
2 hard-boiled eggs, sliced
2 slices onion, chopped
Salt and pepper to taste
½ pound bacon, cut in pieces

¾ cup wine or cider vinegar
¼ cup water
1 tablespoon flour
3 tablespoons sugar
¼ cup water

Slice cooled potatoes. Mix with sliced eggs, onion, salt and pepper. Fry bacon until crisp, remove with slotted spoon, and drain on paper. Stir into potato mixture. Stir vinegar and first ¼ cup water into bacon fat in pan and bring to boil. Combine flour, sugar, and second ¼ cup water to make a smooth paste, then stir into boiling vinegar mixture. Stir, boiling, until sauce thickens slightly. Add to potato mixture and stir gently to blend. Refrigerate until ready to use. About half an hour before serving, heat salad in 325°F. oven, stirring occasionally. Serves 6-8.

MAINE MANSION HOT POTATO SALAD

More quickly made than the preceding salad.

3 medium potatoes, cooked and
  cubed, hot
4 slices bacon
⅓ cup chopped onion
¼ cup wine vinegar

1 teaspoon sugar
Salt and pepper to taste
1 egg, beaten
2 hard-boiled eggs, chopped
2 tablespoons chopped fresh parsley

Keep cubed potatoes warm. Fry bacon, remove with slotted spoon, drain, and crumble over potatoes. Cook onion in bacon fat until translucent. Add vinegar, sugar, salt and pepper, and stir to blend. Remove from heat and stir in beaten egg. Pour over potatoes and bacon and stir to blend. Add chopped egg and stir in gently. Garnish with parsley and serve. Serves 6.

CASSEROLE POTATO SALAD

A spicy salad sparked with touches of holiday color.

4 slices bacon
6 medium potatoes, cooked and
   cubed
½ cup chopped pimiento
¼ cup chopped onion

1½ cups chopped celery
1 clove garlic, minced
Salt to taste
Hot dressing (see below)

Preheat oven to 350°F. Cook bacon until crisp, drain, and crumble. Reserve fat to use in dressing. In 1½-quart casserole, combine all ingredients except dressing. Pour dressing (below) over mixture. Heat in oven for 30 minutes, or until thoroughly heated. Serves 6-8.

Hot Dressing:

4 tablespoons melted bacon fat
4 tablespoons wine vinegar
1 clove garlic, crushed

1 teaspoon basil, crushed
½ teaspoon dry mustard
Salt and pepper to taste

Combine all ingredients in small saucepan. Bring to boil, stirring, and pour over potato mixture.

SKILLET SALAD

Cheese makes the difference here. A good luncheon dish.

3 medium potatoes, sliced or cubed
2 tablespoons butter
1 12-ounce can luncheon meat, cut
   into 2x½-inch strips
¼ cup chopped onion

¼ cup chopped green pepper
¼ cup French dressing
1½ cups American or cheddar
   cheese, diced

Sauté potatoes in butter in skillet until tender and brown. Add meat, onion, and green pepper. Cook until meat is hot and onion and green pepper are tender. Turn heat to low. Pour in dressing and stir gently to blend. Add cheese and continue cooking until cheese melts slightly. Serve immediately. Serves 4-6.

BREADS AND BREADSTUFFS

In this section, we have included in order of appearance: muffins, biscuits, rolls, breads, waffles, doughnuts, pancakes made from grated raw potatoes and pancakes made from mashed potatoes, dumplings, and stuffings.

Potato Breads
(Waffles and Doughnuts, Too)

MUFFINS

Potatoes make these among the world's tenderest.

2 tablespoons butter
2 tablespoons sugar, or 1 tablespoon
   honey
1 egg, beaten
1 cup mashed potatoes

2 cups sifted flour
3 teaspoons baking powder
½ teaspoon salt
1 cup milk

Preheat oven to 350°F. Cream butter with sugar or honey, then beat in egg and potatoes. Blend well. Sift dry ingredients together and add alternately with milk to potato mixture. Continue beating until smooth. Fill greased or papered muffin tins two-thirds full and bake 25 to 30 minutes, until nicely browned. Makes 12 muffins.

ONIONY POTATO MUFFINS

These are terrific dinner muffins.

2 eggs, separated
3 cups grated raw potatoes
¼ cup grated onion
½ cup flour

½ teaspoon salt
½ teaspoon baking powder
3 tablespoons melted butter

Preheat oven to 400°F. Beat egg yolks until light yellow. Press excess moisture out of potatoes and combine with yolks. Stir to blend. Add in onion, flour, salt, baking powder, and butter. Beat egg whites until stiff and fold into batter. Spoon batter into greased muffin tins, filling them two-thirds full. Bake 20 to 25 minutes. Makes 12 muffins.

CHICAGO POTATO-FLOUR MUFFINS

Light as air.

4 eggs, separated
¼ teaspoon salt
1 tablespoon sugar, or 2 teaspoons
   honey

½ cup potato flour
1 teaspoon baking powder
2 tablespoons ice water

Preheat oven to 375°F. Combine egg whites and salt and beat until very stiff. Beat yolks in separate bowl, and beat in sugar or honey until mixture is thick and lemon-colored. Sift flour and baking powder. Combine flour mixture with yolks, stirring gently, then lightly fold in egg whites. Gently stir in ice water. Spoon into greased muffin tins and bake 15 to 20 minutes. Makes 12 muffins.

POTATO PUDDING PUFFS

Crusty on the outside, moist on the inside.

3 medium potatoes, finely grated
1 egg, beaten
1 small onion, finely grated

½ teaspoon salt
¼ teaspoon baking powder
Pepper

Preheat oven to 350°F. Press potatoes against fine strainer to remove as much water as possible. Combine with remaining ingredients and stir to blend. Spoon into 9 greased muffin cups, filling each cup two-thirds full. Bake for 40 to 45 minutes, until gently puffed and brown. Serve piping hot. Makes 9 puffs.

POTATO SCONES

Traditional and delicious Scottish afternoon-tea fare, these are especially good served hot with butter and honey or strawberry jam.

⅓ cup butter
1 cup mashed potatoes
1½ cups flour
½ teaspoon salt

4 teaspoons baking powder
2 tablespoons sugar
½ cup milk
(½ cup currants or raisins)

Preheat oven to 400°F. Combine butter and mashed potatoes. Combine dry ingredients including sugar, and sift over potatoes. Pour in milk and optional currants or raisins, and mix all together just enough to moisten flour. Turn dough out onto floured board and knead 15 times. Shape dough into an 8-inch round, 1 inch thick, and score into 8 wedges. Place on ungreased cookie sheet and bake about 20 minutes, until lightly browned. Makes 8 scones.

POTATO BISCUITS

An airy version of basic baking powder biscuits.

1 medium potato, peeled and boiled	½ teaspoon salt
¾ cup flour	1 tablespoon butter
1 tablespoon baking powder	6 tablespoons milk

Preheat oven to 400°F. Mash or rice potato and set aside. In large bowl, combine flour, baking powder, and salt. Cut in butter with pastry blender or two knives. Stir in potato, then add milk, blending lightly until flour is barely moistened. Shape into 12 biscuits on greased cookie sheet. Bake 15 to 20 minutes, until biscuits are golden. Makes 12 biscuits.

POTATO ROLLS

Tender and light, these rolls are always popular. The dough also does well shaped into a loaf and baked at 350°F. for 30 minutes.

¾ cup potato cooking water	½ teaspoon salt
1 package active dry yeast	1 cup mashed potatoes
¼ cup sugar	3½ cups flour
¼ cup melted butter	

Heat potato water to lukewarm and stir yeast into it until dissolved. In large bowl, combine dissolved yeast, sugar, butter, and salt and stir together. Add potatoes and blend well. Stir in 1 cup flour. Cover and let rise in warm place for 1 hour. Stir in more flour to form stiff dough. Turn dough out on floured board and knead until smooth and elastic. Place in greased bowl and let rise, covered, until doubled in bulk (about 45 minutes). Form dough into 16 balls and place loosely in greased 9 x 9-inch pan. Cover and let rise for 30 minutes. Preheat oven to 425°F. and bake rolls for 10 to 15 minutes, until golden. Makes 16 rolls.

RICH POTATO ROLLS

Eggs and milk make these tender items extra-nourishing.

½ cup mashed potatoes	1 package active dry yeast
⅔ cup butter	½ cup lukewarm water
½ cup sugar, or ¼ cup honey	1 cup warm milk
1 teaspoon salt	6 to 8 cups flour
2 eggs, beaten	

Combine and blend potatoes, butter, sugar or honey, and salt. Stir in eggs. Dissolve yeast in water and combine with milk. Blend liquids into potato mixture. Stir in flour to form stiff dough. Turn dough out onto floured board and knead until smooth and elastic. Place in greased bowl, cover, and let rise in warm place until doubled in bulk (about 1 hour). Punch dough down and shape into walnut-sized rolls. Place in greased baking pans or buttered muffin tins and let rise again until doubled, about 1½ hours. Bake at 400°F. for 15 to 20 minutes. Makes about 3 dozen rolls.

WHOLE WHEAT POTATO BREAD

Marvelously textured brown loaves.

2 packages active dry yeast
½ cup warm water
2 cups milk or water
1 cup mashed potatoes
½ cup wheat germ
2 tablespoons sugar, brown sugar, or honey

2 tablespoons softened butter or cooking oil
½ teaspoon salt
3 cups white flour
3 cups whole wheat flour

Dissolve yeast in warm water. In large bowl, combine 2 cups milk or water, potatoes, wheat germ, sweetener, butter or oil, and salt. Add yeast and white flour, and stir vigorously for 3 minutes. Stir in whole wheat flour, adding additional white flour to make a stiff dough if necessary. Turn dough out on floured board and knead until smooth and elastic (about 10 minutes). Place dough in bowl and coat with oil, turning to coat all surfaces. Cover with towel, put in warm draft-free place and let rise until doubled in bulk (about 1 hour). Punch dough down, shape into 2 loaves, and bake either in 2 greased 9x5-inch loaf pans or on greased baking sheet. Bake at 350°F. for 30 to 40 minutes, until loaves are brown and test done. Cool on wire racks. Makes 2 loaves.

RUSSIAN BLACK BREAD

Make this with or without caraway seed and serve as the outside of a corned beef sandwich or the "beside" of borscht, cabbage soup, or sausage stew.

2 packages active dry yeast
½ cup warm water
2 cups milk
2 tablespoons dark molasses
2 tablespoons Postum powder (or instant coffee, or other coffee substitute)

1 ounce baking chocolate, melted
1 teaspoon salt
1 cup mashed potatoes
(1 tablespoon caraway seed)
½ cup whole bran cereal
3½ cups all-purpose flour
2½ cups rye flour

Dissolve yeast in warm water. Warm milk slightly and place it in large bowl. Add molasses, Postum, chocolate, and salt. Stir to blend, cool to lukewarm, and add yeast. Stir in mashed potatoes, optional caraway seed, whole bran cereal, and all-purpose flour. Stir vigorously to blend ingredients and develop gluten. Stir in rye flour to form a stiff dough. Turn dough out on lightly floured board and knead until dough becomes smooth and elastic (10 to 15 minutes). Rub all surfaces of dough with margarine or cooking oil, place dough in bowl, cover, and let rise in warm place until nearly doubled in bulk (about 1 hour). Punch down dough and let sit for 5 minutes. Shape dough into 2 round or oblong loaves and place on greased baking sheet. Let rise again until nearly doubled in bulk (about 45 minutes). Bake at 350°F. for 35 to 45 minutes, until loaves test done. Brush tops with salt water (1½ teaspoons salt dissolved in ½ cup water) during baking for thicker crust. Remove finished loaves from oven and cool on wire rack. Makes 2 loaves.

POTATO SWEET DOUGH

Use this as you would sweet bread (coffee-cake) dough, spreading it with melted butter and jam or nuts and cinnamon, rolling it up, and slicing it into rolls.

1 package active dry yeast
½ cup lukewarm water
1 cup milk
½ cup butter
½ cup sugar

½ teaspoon salt
1 cup mashed potatoes
2 eggs, beaten
4 to 5 cups flour

Stir yeast into warm water and let sit for about 5 minutes. Scald milk and combine with butter, sugar, salt, and potatoes in large bowl. Stir in eggs. Add yeast and stir in enough flour to make a stiff dough. Knead on a lightly floured board until smooth and elastic. Place in greased bowl, turning dough to grease all sides, and cover tightly. Place in refrigerator 8 hours or longer, (or let rise for 1 hour in a warm place and shape into rolls). About 1½ to 2 hours before baking remove dough from refrigerator and shape or fill as desired. Bake on greased sheets or pans. Bake at 400°F., 15 to 20 minutes. Makes 2 dozen rolls.

POTATO WAFFLES

Substantial version of the ever-popular waffle. Try these also as a base for creamed chicken or ham.

2 eggs, separated
1 cup sour milk or buttermilk
1½ cups mashed potatoes
⅓ cup melted butter

1 cup flour
½ teaspoon baking soda
½ teaspoon salt

Beat egg yolks until thick and lemon-colored, and then beat in milk, potatoes, and butter. Sift together dry ingredients and stir into potato mixture. Beat until smooth. Beat egg whites until stiff and gently fold into batter. Bake in preheated waffle iron until crisp and brown. Serve topped with butter and maple syrup. Makes 8 small or 6 medium waffles.

POTATO DOUGHNUTS

Tender lightness inside, crispy crunchiness outside.

3 cups flour
3½ teaspoons baking powder
½ teaspoon salt
½ teaspoon nutmeg
2 eggs
1 cup sugar

1 cup warm mashed potatoes
3 tablespoons bacon fat or melted
  butter
¼ cup milk
Fat for deep frying

Sift together dry ingredients. Beat eggs well, then beat in sugar, potato, and bacon fat or melted butter. Beat thoroughly. Gently stir in milk, then add dry ingredients and stir until flour is barely moistened. Chill in refrigerator 1 hour or longer. Divide dough and roll out both halves on floured cloth. Cut with floured doughnut cutter and fry in deep fat (350°F.) until golden. Turn once while frying so both sides brown evenly. Roll in confectioners', granulated, or cinnamon sugar. Makes 2 dozen.

Potato Pancakes

You can use either grated raw potatoes or mashed potatoes to make pancakes; here are a number of different ways to use each.

KARTOFFEL PFANNKUCHEN

The potato pancake is a way of life in Germany and Scandinavia.

6 medium potatoes
1 small onion, minced
4 slices bacon, fried crisp and
  crumbled
2 tablespoons flour

1 teaspoon salt
⅛ teaspoon nutmeg
Pepper to taste
2 eggs, beaten
2 tablespoons chopped fresh parsley

Peel and grate the potatoes. Soak in cold water for 10 minutes, then drain and press out as much water as possible. Combine with onion, crumbled bacon, flour, and seasonings. Stir in eggs and parsley. Drop batter, ⅓ cup at a time, into hot skillet greased with melted butter. Flatten cakes, brown, and turn to brown on other side. Drain and serve. Makes 12 pancakes.

EXTRA-CRISP PANCAKES

A thinner batter for crisper pancakes. Great topped with cut-up chicken or pork in gravy, and good for breakfast, too.

2 cups grated peeled potatoes
2 eggs, beaten
½ teaspoon salt

1½ tablespoons flour
1 tablespoon minced onion
½ cup milk, brought just to boil

Combine all ingredients and stir to blend thoroughly. Drop onto hot greased griddle or skillet, turning once to brown both sides. Serves 2-4.

MONADNOCK POTATO PANCAKES

Potato pancakes leavened with baking powder.

3 large potatoes
3 teaspoons baking powder
1 cup milk, scalded

½ cup flour
¼ teaspoon salt
2 eggs, well beaten

Peel and grate potatoes. Drain excess water. Stir in remaining ingredients and cook by large spoonfuls on hot greased griddle. Turn to brown both sides. Top with butter and honey or syrup. Serves 3.

BOXTY CAKES

An Irish favorite, these are lighter than most potato cakes — quite like biscuits.

4 medium potatoes
1⅓ cups flour
1 teaspoon salt

1 teaspoon baking powder
⅔ cup milk

Peel and grate potatoes. Sift dry ingredients and combine with potatoes and milk. Stir to blend thoroughly, but do not overbeat. Drop by large spoonfuls onto hot greased griddle and cook about 10 minutes on each side. Cakes will become brown and fluffy. Spread hot cakes with butter and serve. Makes 6-8 cakes.

CARAWAY CRUSTIES

Distinctive caraway-touched pancakes from Germany.

6 medium potatoes
½ teaspoon crushed caraway seed
½ cup milk or light cream

1 egg, beaten
½ teaspoon salt
2 tablespoons flour, or more

Peel and grate potatoes. Combine with other ingredients, adding enough flour to give dough body. Fry in butter or bacon fat over high heat, turning cakes once. Serve immediately. Serves 4-6.

GREEK POTATO PANCAKES

Just about every country has its own particular way with potato pancakes. This is the way they do it in Greece. There, they call them "patatokeftethes." Serve as is, or garnish with yogurt or garlic sauce.

2 cups cold mashed potatoes
2 eggs
1 tablespoon chopped onion
¼ cup flour
1 teaspoon chopped parsley

Salt and pepper to taste
¼ cup grated Parmesan or Greek
  Kefaloteri cheese
Oil for frying or butter for broiling or
  baking

Combine all but cheese and oil or butter in bowl and blend thoroughly. Shape into pancakes, dip in cheese, and fry, bake, or broil, as below. Serves 4-6.

To Bake or Broil: Butter baking pan, lay cakes in it, and bake at 450°F. about 15 minutes until hot and brown. Broil about 10 minutes.

To Fry: Fry on seasoned griddle, turning once, so that both sides are browned.

LLAPINGACHOS

From Peru, native land of the potato. A hearty and sustaining breakfast.

6 medium potatoes
2 tablespoons butter
Salt and pepper to taste
2 tablespoons grated cheddar or
  American cheese

2 tablespoons bacon fat or butter
2 small onions, sliced
3 medium tomatoes, sliced
6 eggs, poached

Peel potatoes and boil until tender, about 20 minutes. Drain potatoes and mash. Add butter and salt and pepper to taste. Stir in cheese and let it melt. Shape mixture into 6 flat cakes. Melt bacon fat or butter in skillet and fry cakes until nicely browned on both sides. Remove and keep warm. Sauté onion in fat or butter in skillet, add tomatoes, and simmer about 15 minutes. Pour over fried cakes and top with a poached egg. Serves 6.

IRISH PRATIE CAKES

Spread with honey or jam and serve with tea (or breakfast!).

4 medium potatoes, peeled
2 tablespoons melted butter

½ teaspoon salt
1¼ cups flour

Cook and mash potatoes. Stir in butter and salt. Knead in flour gradually until dough becomes smooth and elastic. Roll out to ¼-inch thickness and cut into triangles or circles. Cook on griddle over medium heat, 5 to 10 minutes on each side. Cakes should be lightly browned. Makes 6-8 cakes.

IRISH STAMPY CAKES

Lovely and moist. Serve with crisp bacon or with lamb chops.

2 cups hot mashed potatoes
½ cup flour
½ teaspoon salt

1 tablespoon milk
2 tablespoons melted butter
  or bacon fat

Preheat oven to 350°F. Combine ingredients and blend until dough is smooth. Roll out ½ inch thick on floured board and cut into circles. Place on lightly greased cookie sheet and bake 30 minutes, turning once. Makes 8 cakes.

NORWEGIAN LEFAS

Here's how they make potato pancakes east of the sun — in Norway. Either serve with gravy or cream sauce beside poultry or ham, or as a dessert, topped with blueberry or maple syrup.

5 cups hot mashed potatoes
½ cup light cream
1 teaspoon salt

½ cup (1 stick) butter
2½ cups flour

Combine potatoes, cream, salt, and butter, and stir until butter has melted completely. Stir in flour. Chill mixture in refrigerator 2 hours or longer. Form chilled mixture into walnut-sized balls and roll them out to ⅛-inch thickness on lightly floured board. Fry in hot oil or butter in skillet until brown on both sides. The cakes should be crisp. Serves 8-10.

BOXTY-ON-THE-GRIDDLE CAKES

A traditional Irish breakfast, especially on Fridays. Top with butter and honey, applesauce, syrup, or jam.

1 cup grated raw potato
1 cup hot mashed potatoes
1 cup flour
1 teaspoon baking powder

½ teaspoon salt
2 eggs, beaten
¼ cup milk

Combine all ingredients and stir to blend. Add more milk, if necessary, to make dough moderately moist. Drop by large spoonfuls on hot seasoned griddle, let brown, and turn to brown other side. Serve hot. Makes about 12 cakes.

Dumplings and Noodles

POTATO DUMPLINGS

Cook these on top of beef, lamb, veal, or chicken stew for a hearty treat.

2 cups mashed potatoes
1 egg
¼ cup flour
1 tablespoon finely minced onion

1 tablespoon chopped fresh parsley,
or 1 teaspoon dried
½ teaspoon salt

Combine all ingredients in small bowl. Blend well. Drop by spoonfuls onto bubbling stew, cover, and cook 20 minutes. Makes 12 dumplings.

CHEESY DUMPLINGS

Incomparable served plain with hot beef or veal broth poured over them or as dumplings over casseroles.

1 cup mashed potatoes
1½ tablespoons butter
1 egg yolk
2 tablespoons grated Parmesan
cheese

Dash nutmeg
½ teaspoon salt
Fat for deep frying
6 cups beef or veal broth

Combine first 6 ingredients and stir to blend thoroughly. Form into long strips about ½ inch wide and lay out on floured board. Cut into ½-inch pieces and form into balls. Brown in deep fat heated to 365°F. to 380°F. Heat broth separately and pour over dumplings. Serve immediately. Serves 6.

PENNSYLVANIA POTATO DUMPLINGS

Drop these tasty dumplings onto chicken or sauerkraut-and-sausage stew.

6 medium potatoes
10 slices bread
1 teaspoon salt
Pepper to taste

1 medium onion, grated
1 teaspoon minced fresh parsley
2 eggs, well beaten
Flour

Peel and grate potatoes. Cover bread with cold water for 5 minutes, then squeeze out as much as possible. Combine soaked bread, salt, pepper, onion, and parsley. Stir in potatoes and eggs and blend thoroughly. With hands, mold into walnut-sized balls and gently roll in flour. Drop onto stew or boiling salted water. Cover tightly and cook, undisturbed, for 15 minutes. Serves 6.

IRISH POTATO DUMPLINGS

These dress up a roast, and scintillate under gravy.

1 tablespoon minced onion
2 tablespoons butter or bacon fat
½ cup grated raw potato
6 medium boiled potatoes, riced or
    mashed and cooled

1 teaspoon salt
¾ cup flour
2 eggs, beaten

Sauté onion in butter or bacon fat until onion is golden. Drain grated potatoes and add to onion. Cook, stirring, until mixture becomes pasty. Cool, then stir in cooked potatoes and remaining ingredients. Stir until smooth. Form into walnut-sized balls and drop into boiling salted water. Cook about 15 minutes, until dumplings rise to top and are cooked through. Drain and serve. Serves 4-6.

CRISPY BREADED DUMPLINGS

Try these with pork roast, or, for real crunchophiles, with fried chicken.

2 tablespoons butter
1 cup bread cubes
3 medium boiled potatoes, cooled
2 tablespoons flour
1 tablespoon melted butter or
    bacon fat

2 egg yolks, beaten
Salt and pepper
Bread crumbs
Butter or deep fat for frying

Melt 2 tablespoons butter and brown bread cubes in it. Set cubes aside. Peel and mash or rice potatoes and stir flour, butter, yolks, salt and pepper into them. Shape potato dough into walnut-size balls, each having a browned cube of bread in the middle. Cook in boiling water until dumplings rise to surface, about 15 minutes. Drain, roll in bread crumbs, and fry in butter or deep fat until crisp. Drain and serve. Serves 6.

POTATO NOODLES

These noodles are made by the millions in Czechoslovakia, and are well worth the effort.

6 medium potatoes
½ teaspoon salt
3 tablespoons flour

3 eggs
4 tablespoons butter

Boil potatoes in lightly-salted water until tender. Peel and mash while still hot. Stir in salt, flour, and eggs, and knead with fingers to form a soft dough. Add more flour if necessary. Roll out dough on lightly-floured board to ⅛-inch thickness. Cut into noodles 4 inches long and ¼ inch wide. Preheat oven to 370°F. and butter a 1½-quart baking dish. Arrange noodles lattice-fashion in dish and dot with butter. Bake for 30 minutes, or until lightly browned. Serves 6.

Potato Stuffings

MASHED POTATO STUFFING

Unusual stuffing for poultry, lamb, or pork.

3 medium potatoes, peeled, boiled, and mashed
1 tablespoon melted butter
1 medium onion, finely chopped
2 tablespoons chopped fresh parsley, or 1 tablespoon dried

1 tablespoon poultry seasoning
1 teaspoon salt
Pepper
Dash garlic powder

Combine all ingredients in large bowl. Place inside meat and cook, adding 5 minutes per pound to cooking time for unstuffed meat. Serve with meat and gravy. Or place in greased 1-quart baking dish and bake 40 minutes at 375°F. Makes about 2½ cups stuffing.

SAVORY STUFFING

Poultry or veal seem especially perky stuffed with this mixture.

8 medium potatoes
½ cup pork sausage
1 cup chopped onions
½ cup chopped celery
4 tablespoons melted butter
1 cup bread crumbs

½ teaspoon sage
½ teaspoon celery seed
½ teaspoon summer savory
1 teaspoon salt
¼ teaspoon pepper
2 eggs, beaten

Boil, drain, peel, and mash potatoes. Brown sausage, onion, and celery in butter. Combine with other ingredients and blend well. Makes about 6 cups stuffing.

MINTY APPLE STUFFING

Apples lend a sweet touch, mint the piquance, in this stuffing especially good with lamb, but also nice with chicken or turkey.

4 medium potatoes, peeled, boiled, and diced
2 cups (about 4 medium) apples, peeled and diced
½ cup diced celery

1 tablespoon butter
1 teaspoon finely chopped mint, or ¼ teaspoon dried
½ teaspoon salt

Combine all ingredients in large bowl. Bake in greased 1-quart casserole dish in 375°F. oven for 40 minutes, or cook inside meat or poultry, adding 5 minutes per pound to cooking time of roast. Makes about 5 cups.

IRISH POTATO STUFFING

Traditional stuffing for the Christmas goose. Good for a turkey, too!

8 large potatoes, peeled and boiled
4 tablespoons melted butter
  or bacon fat
1 cup finely chopped onion
½ cup diced celery
1 cup coarse bread crumbs

1 teaspoon sage
½ teaspoon celery salt
½ teaspoon thyme
1 teaspoon salt
Pepper to taste
2 eggs, beaten

Rice or mash potatoes, and combine with remaining ingredients. Blend well. Enough stuffing to fill a 10-pound goose, or a 12- to 14-pound turkey.

PENNSYLVANIA DUTCH POTATO "FILLING"

Particularly designed for roast pork.

1 small onion, chopped fine
3 tablespoons butter
½ cup chopped celery
3 tablespoons chopped fresh parsley,
  or 1 tablespoon dried

1½ cups mashed potato
1 cup bread crumbs
1 teaspoon salt
Pepper to taste

Sauté onion in butter until soft, then add celery and continue cooking for 1 minute. Add parsley. Combine with potato in bowl, then stir in bread crumbs, salt, and pepper. Mix well. Spread in greased 9x13-inch pan and top with thin loin chops or loin roast. Roast as usual for pork. Or cook stuffing separately in greased 1-quart dish for 40 minutes at 400°F. until top is brown. Serves 4 or 5.

PORK POTATO STUFFING

The caraway seed in this stuffing adds a delicious flavor to the pork.

5 large potatoes
1 medium onion, grated
1 teaspoon caraway seed

1 tablespoon fresh parsley, minced
1 tablespoon melted butter

Boil, drain, peel, and mash potatoes. Stir in remaining ingredients and blend well. Use to stuff pork chops, or bake 25 minutes at 350°F. and serve with pork roast. Makes about 5 cups stuffing.

POTATO DESSERTS

Yes, it's true — wonderful desserts owe their existence to the humble spud. In this chapter you'll find Pies, Pie Crust, Puddings, Cakes, Cookies, and Candy all deriving their special quality from one common ingredient — the Potato.

Potato Pies

POTATO CUSTARD PIE

Potato enhances the texture of the custard without affecting the taste.

1 medium potato	½ cup milk
2 tablespoons butter	Juice and grated rind of 1 lemon
¾ cup sugar	2 egg whites, beaten stiff
2 egg yolks, beaten	Unbaked 9-inch pie shell (see p. 129)

Preheat oven to 400°F. Peel, boil, drain, and mash potato. Stir in butter and sugar and continue stirring until consistency is creamy. Cool slightly, then beat in egg yolks, milk, and lemon juice and rind, blending thoroughly. Gently fold in beaten egg whites and pour mixture into pastry shell. Bake for about 25 minutes, until crust is done and filling is firm. Serves 6-8.

SARATOGA APPLE PIE

Apple pie sparked with a chips-and-cheese topping.

8 to 10 cooking apples, peeled,
  cored, and sliced
¾ cup sugar
3 tablespoons cornstarch
1 tablespoon lemon juice
1 teaspoon cinnamon or nutmeg

¼ cup flour
¼ cup brown sugar, packed
1 cup grated cheddar cheese
¾ cup crushed potato chips
Unbaked 9-inch pie shell (see p. 129)

Preheat oven to 400°F. Combine apples, sugar, cornstarch, lemon juice, and spice. In a second bowl, blend together flour, brown sugar, cheese, and crushed chips. Turn apple mixture into pie shell. Sprinkle apples evenly with chips mixture. Bake 40 to 50 minutes, or until apples are tender. Check during baking so that if topping becomes brown before apples are cooked, you can lay aluminum foil loosely over top of pie. Serve warm with cream or ice cream. Serves 6-8.

POTATO APPLE CAKE

Despite its name, this is an old-fashioned, and old-favorite apple pie, *full of ginger!*

4 large potatoes
2 tablespoons butter
1 tablespoon sugar
¼ teaspoon ginger
¾ cup sifted flour

4 medium cooking apples, peeled
  and sliced thin
Butter
½ cup brown sugar

Preheat oven to 425°F. Peel potatoes and cook in boiling water until tender. Drain and mash. Stir in butter, sugar, and ginger and blend well. Stir in flour and blend well. Divide the dough in half and roll each half into an 8-inch round. Place 1 round in a greased 8-inch pie plate and spread apple slices on top. Moisten edges of dough and top apples with second round. Pinch edges together and cut several decorative slits in top. Bake for 25 to 30 minutes, until top crust is nicely browned. Remove cake from oven and *carefully* cut close to edge of top crust. Lift off crust, lavish apples with dollops of butter and sprinkle with brown sugar. Carefully replace crust and return cake to oven for another 5 minutes, until butter and sugar have melted completely. Serve piping hot, with cream if desired. Serves 6.

POTATO-BASED PIE SHELL

Pack this moist crust with a sweet filling, or reduce sugar to ½ teaspoon and use for main-dish pies.

1 cup flour, sifted before measuring
½ teaspoon salt
1 tablespoon sugar

½ cup cold mashed potatoes
⅓ cup butter

Preheat oven to 400°F. Sift together dry ingredients. With a pastry blender or fork, cut in potatoes to form a coarse meal. Cut in butter. Make dough into a ball, wrap tightly, and refrigerate for half an hour. Remove dough from wrap, roll out on floured board, and use to line an 8- or 9-inch pie pan.

Either fill before baking, and bake 40 to 45 minutes, or until filling is done, or prick bottom and sides and bake unfilled shell for 10-12 minutes until lightly browned. Then cool crust before adding filling. Double the recipe and there will be sufficient dough for a 9- or 10-inch 2-crust pie.

Puddings

ALMOND POTATO PUDDING

A light flavor, some custard — not too sweet.

4 eggs, separated
1 cup grated boiled potato
¼ cup sugar
¼ cup ground blanched almonds

3 tablespoons lemon juice
1 teaspoon grated lemon rind
¼ teaspoon salt

Preheat oven to 350°F. Beat egg yolks until thick and lemon-colored. In separate bowl, beat egg whites until stiff. Into yolks, beat all ingredients *except* whites. Fold in egg whites. Grease 1-quart casserole and pour mixture into it. Set in pan of hot water and bake about 45 minutes, until center tests done. Top with sweetened fruit and cream. Serves 6-8.

STEAMED POTATO PUDDING

A memorable Christmas fiesta.

2 tablespoons butter
2 tablespoons suet
½ cup sugar
2 tablespoons molasses
⅓ cup grated raw potato
⅓ cup grated raw carrot
1 small grated raw apple
1¼ cups sifted flour
½ teaspoon baking soda

¼ teaspoon salt
¼ teaspoon nutmeg
¼ teaspoon allspice
¼ teaspoon cinnamon
⅛ teaspoon cloves
½ cup raisins
2 tablespoons chopped citron
¼ cup chopped pecans or walnuts
1 tablespoon chopped candied ginger

Cream butter, suet, and sugar. Beat in molasses, potato, carrot, and apple. Sift together flour, soda, salt, and spices, then mix with remaining ingredients. Blend into creamed mixture. Fill greased and floured pudding mold (1-pound coffee can is ideal) ⅔ full. Cover with foil tied on with string; place mold on rack in heavy pan containing 1 inch boiling water. Steam pan, tightly covered, over medium heat for 3 hours, replenishing water as needed. Serve with hard sauce or whipped cream. Serves 6-8.

Cakes

CHEESECAKE WITH CHIPPY CRUST

Crust that's just right for the cake inside.

Crust:

2 cups finely crushed potato chips
2 tablespoons melted butter

¼ cup confectioners' sugar
1 tablespoon grated lemon peel

Filling:

1½ pounds cream cheese, softened
1 pound ricotta cheese
¼ cup whipping cream
1¾ cups granulated sugar

3 tablespoons flour
1 tablespoon grated lemon peel
1 teaspoon vanilla
6 eggs

Preheat oven to 500°F. Combine ingredients for crust and mix thoroughly. Press into bottom and halfway up sides of 9-inch spring-form pan.

Prepare filling. In large mixing bowl, beat together cream cheese, ricotta, cream, sugar, flour, peel, and vanilla. Beat until mixture is light and fluffy. Beat in eggs, 1 at a time, beating until smooth after each addition.

Pour mixture into crust. Bake at 500°F. for 10 minutes, then reduce heat to 250°F. and bake 60 minutes longer, or until cake is set. Remove from oven, cool, then chill. Carefully remove side of pan. Sprinkle with confectioners' sugar or grated lemon peel and serve. Serves 8-10.

POTATO FRUITCAKE

This makes a moist, rich layer cake, superb topped with vanilla icing.

1 cup butter
2 cups brown sugar, packed
4 eggs
1 cup warm mashed potatoes
2 cups flour
1 teaspoon soda
1 teaspoon baking powder
1 teaspoon salt

1 teaspoon cinnamon
½ teaspoon nutmeg
½ cup cocoa
1 cup raisins
1 cup chopped nuts, pecans or
   walnuts
½ cup milk

Preheat oven to 350°F. Cream butter and brown sugar until light and fluffy. Beat in eggs and potatoes. Sift together dry ingredients and stir in nuts and raisins. Beat into butter mixture alternately with milk. Bake in two 9-inch greased and floured layer pans, for 35 to 40 minutes, until layers test done. Cool on rack, then frost or glaze as desired. Serves 10-12.

MORAVIAN SUGAR CAKE

A luscious coffee cake deeply blessed with rich pockets of brown sugar.

1 cup hot mashed potatoes
1 cup white sugar
1 cup melted butter
1 teaspoon salt
5 cups sifted flour
2 packages dry yeast

1 cup lukewarm water
2 eggs, beaten
1 cup brown sugar
4 tablespoons melted butter
1 teaspoon cinnamon mixed with
   2 tablespoons sugar

Combine potatoes, sugar, butter, and salt in large bowl. Stir in 1 cup flour. Dissolve yeast in 1 cup warm water and add to potato mixture. Stir in half of remaining flour, then half of beaten eggs. Repeat with second half of each. Cover bowl and let rise overnight. In the morning, turn out on floured board and knead lightly. Butter a 9x13-inch baking pan and spread dough in it.

Let rise until doubled in bulk, then punch 12 deep holes in dough, spacing them evenly. Fill each hole with brown sugar mixed with 2 tablespoons melted butter. Drizzle remaining 2 tablespoons melted butter over cake and sprinkle with cinnamon-sugar mixture. Bake in 375°F. oven for 30 minutes, or until cake tests done. Serves 12.

INDIVIDUAL POTATO APPLE CAKES

Traditional All Saints' fare in Ireland.

½ cup sifted flour
¼ teaspoon salt
¼ teaspoon baking powder
1 tablespoon melted butter

1 cup mashed potatoes
2 tart cooking apples
Honey
Melted butter

Sift together dry ingredients. Combine melted butter and potatoes, then stir in dry ingredients and blend thoroughly. Roll dough out on floured board to ¼-inch thickness. Peel and core apples and cut each into 3 rings ½ inch thick. Cut 12 rounds of dough, slightly larger than the apple rings. Top six rounds with a slice of apple each. Dampen edges of dough, top with a second round of dough, and pinch edges together. Fry the rounds in a lightly greased skillet until golden on both sides. Cut a small opening in the top of each round, fill with melted butter and honey, and serve hot. Or sprinkle with sugar while hot and serve. Makes 6 cakes.

PRESQUE ISLE CHOCOLATE CAKE

A light chocolate cake that's a long-time tradition in northern Maine.

2 cups sugar
⅔ cup shortening
4 eggs
1 teaspoon vanilla
1 cup unseasoned hot mashed
  potatoes
2 cups sifted flour

½ cup cocoa
3 teaspoons baking powder
1 teaspoon each cinnamon and
  nutmeg
½ teaspoon salt
½ cup milk

Preheat oven to 350°F. Cream sugar and shortening. Beat in eggs, 1 at a time, beating each in thoroughly. Beat in vanilla and mashed potatoes. Sift together dry ingredients and beat into egg mixture alternately with milk. Bake in two greased 9-inch layer pans for 40 to 50 minutes, or in a greased 9x13-inch baking pan for about 50 minutes. Serves 8-10.

AIR-BORNE DEVIL'S FOOD CAKE

This rich and airy chocolate cake is extra smooth and moist thanks to its mystery ingredient — potato.

½ cup milk
3 ounces baking chocolate
1 cup hot mashed potatoes
1 cup butter
1¾ cups sugar
4 eggs, separated

1½ teaspoons vanilla
2 cups sifted flour
3 teaspoons baking powder
¼ teaspoon salt
¼ cup sugar

Preheat oven to 350°F. Heat milk with chocolate in top of double boiler until chocolate is melted. Stir into mashed potatoes and blend well. Cream butter and sugar until light and fluffy and combine with chocolate mixture. Beat in egg yolks. Stir in vanilla. Sift flour, baking powder, and salt together and stir slowly into chocolate mixture. Beat egg whites until stiff, then gradually beat in ¼ cup sugar to form stiff meringue. Fold meringue gently into batter. Bake in three 8-inch layer cake pans, greased and floured, or in two 9- or 10-inch layers. Bake 25 to 30 minutes, until layers test done. Cool slightly and turn out on racks. Frost cake when cool with vanilla or chocolate frosting, or with whipped cream. Serves 10-12.

GERMAN CHOCOLATE POTATO CAKE

Light, spicy, and really zippy!

¾ cup butter, softened
2 cups white sugar, or 1 cup white
  and 1 cup light brown
4 eggs, separated
1½ cups flour
1 teaspoon cinnamon
¼ teaspoon cloves
2 teaspoons baking powder

½ cup cream
4 ounces baking chocolate, melted
1 teaspoon vanilla
1 tablespoon grated lemon rind
1 cup fresh mashed potatoes, or
  1 cup grated raw potatoes
(1 cup chopped walnuts)

Preheat oven to 325°F. Cream butter and sugar until light and fluffy. Beat in yolks, one at a time, and beat until thoroughly blended. Sift dry ingredients twice and add alternately with cream to egg mixture. Beat in chocolate, vanilla, lemon rind, potatoes, and optional nuts. In separate bowl, beat egg whites until stiff. Fold gently into batter. Bake in greased 9-inch round pan, or in 9-inch spring-form pan. Bake about an hour and a half, until cake tests done. Let cool, then frost with a light chocolate icing. Makes one 9-inch cake.

VANILLA POTATO CAKE

Thanks to the potato, moist and yummy; double the recipe to make a big two-layer birthday cake.

¾ cup butter
1½ cups sugar
4 eggs, separated
1 cup freshly mashed potatoes
1 teaspoon vanilla
2 cups flour

2 teaspoons baking powder
½ teaspoon salt
½ cup milk or cream
½ cup sugar
(1 cup chopped pecans or almonds)

Preheat oven to 350°F. Cream butter until light and beat in 1½ cups sugar. Beat in egg yolks, 1 at a time, blending each yolk well. Beat in potatoes and vanilla. Sift together flour, baking powder, and salt, and add to potato mixture alternately with milk or cream. Stir in optional nuts. Beat egg whites until stiff, then beat in ½ cup sugar. Fold gently into batter. Bake in greased and floured 10-inch round pan, or in 10-inch spring-form pan. Bake 60 to 70 minutes, until cake is lightly browned and tests done. Cool on wire rack and ice with vanilla frosting. Makes one 10-inch cake.

Cookies and Candy

POTATO HERMITS

Just about the best hermits you've ever tasted.

1 cup molasses	1 teaspoon cinnamon
¾ cup butter	½ teaspoon cloves
1½ cups hot mashed potatoes	½ teaspoon nutmeg
2 cups flour, pre-sifted	½ teaspoon ginger
2 teaspoons baking powder	½ cup raisins
½ teaspoon baking soda	½ cup broken pecans or walnuts
½ teaspoon salt	2 tablespoons sugar

Preheat oven to 325°F. Put molasses and butter in saucepan and heat until butter melts. Stir in potatoes. Sift together dry ingredients and stir into molasses mixture. Stir in raisins and nuts. Spread on greased cookie sheets, or drop on greased sheets by spoonfuls. Sprinkle with sugar. Bake 15 to 20 minutes, or until hermits test done. Score spread dough into 2x4-inch pieces and cool on sheets. Then break along score-lines. Remove cookies from pans to wire racks and let cool. Store in tightly-sealed container. About 2 dozen bars or 4 dozen cookies.

POTATO CHIP COOKIES

Bake as one large cookie so everyone can break off some, or as smaller cookies.

2⅔ cups flour	1 cup butter
3 teaspoons baking powder	2 tablespoons lemon juice
1 cup sugar	1 tablespoon water
1 cup finely crushed potato chips	⅛ teaspoon almond extract
1 cup ground toasted almonds	(1 cup chocolate bits)
1 tablespoon grated lemon peel	

Preheat oven to 350°F. Blend flour, baking powder, sugar, chips, almonds, and lemon peel in large bowl. Cut in butter with fork or pastry blender until mixture resembles coarse meal. Lightly stir in remaining ingredients to form a crumbly mixture. Either spread mixture on a greased 12-inch round pan, or drop by generous spoonfuls onto greased cookie sheet. Bake large round for 50 to 60 minutes, smaller cookies about 20 minutes, or until nicely browned. Cool completely on rack, then wrap tightly in airtight wrap and store 12 hours or more before serving. Makes 1 large cookie or 2 dozen small ones.

NUTTY POTATO CANDY

Substitute vanilla, almond, or maple extract for the lemon, and obtain different-tasting candies.

¾ cup mashed potatoes
1½ cups sugar
1 teaspoon lemon extract

1 cup corn- or wheat-flake cereal
1 cup chopped nuts (almonds,
    walnuts, pecans, or peanuts)

Slowly work mashed potatoes into sugar, blending thoroughly. Work in remaining ingredients until evenly blended. Spread in buttered 9x9-inch pan. Cover and let stand at room temperature for 24 hours, then cut into 1-inch squares, and enjoy. Makes 81 squares.

MOCK MARZIPAN

Color small sections of candy, and form into shapes — yellow pears, red apples, orange carrots, or what you will. Or make shapes first and use a brush to paint with food coloring as desired.

2 cups sifted confectioners' sugar
¼ cup mashed potatoes
½ pound blanched almonds, or
    7-ounce package almond paste

1 egg white
1 tablespoon lemon juice
½ teaspoon almond extract

Combine sugar and potatoes and blend thoroughly. Make blanched almonds into paste in blender or crumble almond paste and stir into potato mixture. Add remaining ingredients and blend well. Knead with hands until candy is smooth. Color or shape as desired. Makes about 1 pound candy.

SEACOAST COCONUT CANDY

The bitter chocolate topping contrasts perfectly with the sweet base. A famous Maine treat.

⅓ cup cold mashed potatoes
2 cups confectioners' sugar
1 tablespoon butter
2 cups shredded coconut

1 teaspoon vanilla
¼ teaspoon salt
2 ounces baking chocolate

Combine potatoes and sugar. Stir in butter, coconut, vanilla, and salt and blend thoroughly. Spread in ungreased 9x13-inch pan. Melt chocolate and drizzle over fondant. Let candy set until firm, then cut into 1-inch squares. For an added attraction, divide the fondant into sections before spreading in pan, and color each section with a different color food coloring. Makes 117 one-inch squares.

INDEX

ABOUT THE AUTHOR

If *Mary Cornog* lived in England rather than *New* England, she would be referred to in print as: Mary Wood Cornog, A.B., M.A., Ph.D. "A.B." because that's what the English call our American B.A., which Mary got from Wellesley College; she was awarded her Master of Arts in Greek Language and Literature by Columbia University, and the Ph.D by Boston University in Classical Studies — Greek again, which she reads, writes and teaches fluently. She has also taught Greek, Latin, Greek literature in translation and Ancient and Medieval History at The Dublin School, in Dublin, New Hampshire, where her husband is Headmaster.

Why is a classical scholar writing about gardening and cooking? Well, Mary was brought up and still lives in the country and has been gardening and cooking all her life — starting long before she discovered classical Greece at college. She grows all her own vegetables and flowers, and, of course, her own potatoes! In addition, she writes for *Yankee* Magazine, *The Old Farmer's Almanac,* and other publications, cooks for her family and visiting notables, and takes care of a menagerie of one dog, one horse, five cats, two rabbits, and five chickens. Daughter Sarah, aged eight, is her favorite gardening companion.